"Power to the People! is absolute dynamite. Whether you're young or old, a beginner or an elite athlete, training in your room or in the most high tech facility, if there was only one book I could recommend to help you reach your ultimate physical potential, this would be it. I only wish I'd had a book like this when I first began training.

Showing you how to make do with the cheapest, most basic equipment—a barbell and a dumbbell—Pavel distills the complex science of strength into a humorous, inspiring and above-all practical blueprint for rapid strength gain. Follow his program for three months and you'll not only be amazed but hooked—especially if you are a hardgainer. Expect to build or reinforce a muscular foundation that will serve you in any sport or for any purpose —for the rest of your life.

Simple, concise and truly reader friendly, this amazing book contains it all— everything you need to know—what exercises (only two!), how to do them (unique detailed information you'll find no where else), and why. Power to the People is the ultimate program for "Everyman" —AND Woman! It is the best single source on safe and effective lifting techniques I've ever seen. Follow its advice and, believe it or not, you'll be stronger and more injury-resistant immediately. I guarantee it.

I thought I knew a lot, with my Ph.D. and 40 years of training experience—but I learned a heck of a lot and it's improved my training significantly."
—*Jim Wright, Ph.D., Science Editor, Flex Magazine, Weider Group*

"Pavel Tsatsouline has burst onto the American health and fitness scene like a Russian cyclone. He razes the sacred temples of fitness complacency and smugness with his revolutionary concepts and ideas. If you want tired rhetoric and a feel-good approach to fitness look elsewhere. If you want a new and innovative approach to the age old dilemma of physical transformation, you've struck the mother-lode."
—*Marty Gallagher, Coach, Team USA, 1991 world powerlifting champions, World masters powerlifting champion, Editor, Parrillo Performance Press*

"Pavel and his book are the best imports from Russia since Siberian Ginseng! A fountain of information... an elixir for the body."
—*Fairfax Hackley, Arnold Schwarzenegger Classic Martial Arts Seminar Director*

" Pavel Tsatsouline reveals an authentically Russian approach to physical fitness. He shows how anyone, by learning to contract their muscles harder, can build up incredible levels of strength without gaining an ounce of weight. *Power to the People!* is a highly recommended addition to any personal or professional physical fitness reference bookshelf."—*The Bookwatch, Midwest Book Review.*

"I learned a lot from Pavel's books and plan to use many of his ideas in my own workouts. *Power to the People!* is an eye-opener. It will give you new—and valuable—perspectives on strength training. You will find plenty of ideas here to make your training more productive."—*Clarence Bass, author of Ripped 1, 2 &3.*

"A good book for the athlete looking for a routine that will increase strength without building muscle mass. Good source of variation for anyone who's tired of doing standard exercises."—*Jonathan Lawson, IronMan Magazine*

Russian Strength Training Secrets For Every American

By Pavel Tsatsouline,
Master of Sports

Published in the United States by:
Dragon Door Publications, Inc
P.O. Box 4381, St. Paul, MN 55104
Tel: (651) 645-0517 • Fax: (651) 644-5676
Credit card orders: 1-800-899-5111
Email: dragondoor@aol.com • Website: www.dragondoor.com

ISBN: 0-938045-19-9

Book and cover design, Illustrations and photo effects by Derek Brigham
Website http//www.dbrigham.com • Tel/Fax: (612) 827-3431 • Email: dbrigham@visi.com

Digital photography by Robert Pearl Photography • Tel: (612) 617-7724

Manufactured in the United States
First Edition: January 2000

DISCLAIMER
The author and publisher of this material are not responsible in any manner whatsoever for any injury that may occur through following the instructions in this material. The activities, physical and otherwise, described herein for informational purposes, may be too strenuous or dangerous for some people and the reader should consult a physician before engaging in them.

Russian roads are everything you have heard about them and more. Locals were not surprised when an American cyclist on a mission to cross Siberia got stuck in the middle of Russia's twelve time zones with a busted wheel rim. Because Russian bicycle wheels are bigger than American ones, the dude was going to be parked in the middle of nowhere for weeks waiting for a replacement from California. "Don't sweat!" said a local handyman puffing on an evil Kazbek filterless cigarette. He pulled the

spokes out of a Russian rim, cut it and removed a segment. Then he reshaped and welded it. American spokes went back in, and the foreign adventurer was back on the road!

Russians have always made do with simple solutions without compromising the results. NASA aerospace types say that while America sends men to the moon in a Cadillac, Russia manages to launch them into space in a tin can. Enter the tin can approach to designing a world class body—in your basement with $150 worth of equipment. After all, US gyms are stuffed with hi-tech gear, yet it is the Russians with their metal junkyard training facilities who have dominated the Olympics for decades.

Americans are known for thinking outside the box and in the days when there were no supplements and AbRollers to pedal, they came up with effective strength training methods. Follow the advice of Earle Liederman from his Secrets of Strength published in 1925 and quoted frequently in my book, and you will get results superior to anything you can expect from most of the weight training books on the today's market. Why? –Because if you knew how to train correctly, you would get immediate, satisfying results and would not spend a small fortune on shady supplements and equipment as functional as the looks of a '57 Chevy.

The Commies were not motivated by vitamin sales. They wanted one thing: athletic supremacy. If a method did not work –it was discarded, no matter how attractive it sounded. A straightforward formula for strength has been distilled from the mix of sophisticated research, plain trial and error, and unscrupulous espionage. Many of the techniques recommended in the book originate in countries other than the former Soviet Union, including the US.

Unfazed by laughable considerations of which brand of the leg curl machine is best (they are all worthless). Unadorned by the emotional appeal to your mating instinct. Russian strength training secrets are finally available to an average American who wants to get strong and hard. Without blowing 'evergreens', as Russians call the ever-so-stable US dollars. Without living in the gym. Without delayed gratification.

Pavel "the Evil Russian" Tsatsouline,
August 1999, Minnesota, USA

Dedication

KT. OZR. Malta. Always.

TABLE OF CONTENTS

Wired for power: superstrength without bulk 8
How to install a 'muscle software' upgrade into your nervous system and improve your strength and muscle tone....Why the fascination with bodybuilding has led to a decline in effective strength training.... Futuristic techniques which enable you to squeeze more horse-power out of your body-engine.

Tension! What force is made of 10
How tension generates force.....How to maximize muscular tension for traffic-stopping muscular definition...The five keys to high tension training...The inverse relationship between velocity and strength....Flexing to maximize tension...The function of the mechanoreceptors in regulating strength....Using Henneman's size principle to maximize muscular recruitment....Why high values of fatigue and tension are mutually exclusive.

Training to failure-or to success? 14
Why the strongest men and women in the world have never trained to failure....Why intensity is the single most important factor in strength training....The fallacy of 'pushing to the limit'...The only scientific definition of weight training intensity..... Pushing the limits of weight/tension, not reps/exhaustion.....Why training to muscle failure is counterproductive... Greasing the neural groove using the Hebbian rule.

Don't water down your strength with reps and fatigue! 16
How to minimize various types of fatigue and get the most out of your strength training...How to ensure high energy after your workout....Why performing more than five reps per set hinders strength development....Why you need to increase the rest intervals between sets....Why it's best to do only two sets....Why you need to pause and relax between reps...How to build greater ligament strength by "locking and loading"....Surprising advice on how often to practice a lift for optimal gains.

More low rep advantages 20
Three reasons why heavy low rep training is the safest way to lift.... Why the stabilizing muscles are prematurely fatigued during high-rep sets.... Why most serious injuries occur during fatigued states....Why bodybuilders suffer from more pec tears than powerlifters....the significance of concentration for injury prevention...Low reps for a better quality of life...Why heavy low reps can have a tonic, energizing effect on the nervous system.

Rigor mortis, or why high reps failed to tone you up 22
Why going for the 'burn' doesn't work....What is 'real' muscle tone and how do you get it?.....building muscular tension from neurological activity, not energy exhaustion....Increasing muscle tone through a more alert nervous system...Why strength and tone training is the same thing....why deadlifts work best for steel glutes...How to get maximum definition in your triceps...Why training heavy is the best way to get ripped.

"But I don't want to bulk up!" 24
Why lifting heavy doesn't have to translate into bulking up....What makes a biceps grow?.... How to get stronger and harder without getting bigger...minimizing muscular tear-down and reconstruction.... Increasing your muscles' packing density....Why a denser muscle is a harder muscle.

Paul Anderson. 'The Wonder of Nature'. In 1956 strength experts were convinced that the records set by this three hundred-fifty pound mastodon had announced the end of weightlifting history. Yet at the 1996 Olympics in Atlanta Bulgarian defector Naim Suleimanoglu snatched more weight than legendary 'Big Andy'... at one hundred thirty two pounds soaking wet.

Don't judge a book by its cover. Don't judge a man's strength by the size of his biceps. Things are often not what they appear to be. When it is said that a muscle's strength is proportional to its cross-section, that statement must be qualified: everything else being equal. 'Everything else' is largely the level of activation of the muscles by the nervous system, or *neurological efficiency*. It is estimated that an average person can contract only 20-30% of his muscles when trying his hardest. Even a top lifter uses no more that 50% of his impressive muscles!

Your muscles are *already* capable of lifting a car. They just do not know it yet.

To appreciate your true strength potential, ponder the fact that when a person is electrocuted—by lightning, or the Fed—his muscles tear, his tendons rip off their attachments, even bones break... For the first—and last—time in the death row inmate's or golfer's life his muscles were fully activated by electricity.

Although we do not know yet how to completely overcome the *strength deficit* (which is good—you would rip yourself apart!), modern training methods can dramatically improve your muscle activation—and your strength with it. *Power to the People!* will teach you how to install the top of the line 'muscle software' into your nervous system and improve your strength and muscle tone. Without putting on an ounce of weight if that is your wish.

▼

Function precedes structure.

-Wolff's Law

▲

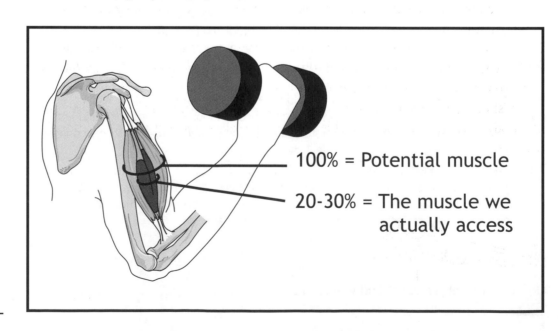

100% = Potential muscle

20-30% = The muscle we actually access

"It is important to note that most of the... factors underlying strength production are functional rather structural," point out top Russian strength expert Prof. Yuri Verkhoshansky and his South African counterpart Dr. Mel Siff. "Those determined by efficiency of the nervous system are of fundamental concern to the development of strength, since the muscular 'motors' are operated by synchronized electrical impulses supplied to the muscles by the nerves. Current preoccupation with the use of anabolic steroids to produce physical bulk thus may be seen to be misplaced, unless bodybuilding bulk is the sole objective. The development of specialized training regimes to enhance nervous system conditioning would be scientifically and morally more advisable..."

In the 1980s hardcore New York powerlifter Dr. Ken Leistner watched the explosion of bodybuilding and predicted the decline of effective strength training. He was right. Proliferation of the strength = size mentality lead to two unfortunate developments.

First, athletes started equating strength training with bodybuilding. The result was 'Hollywood muscle'—all show and no go. Although the new breed of US weightlifters were unquestionably buff, they, unlike their predecessors, could not hold a candle to the Eastern Europeans when it came to hoisting iron.

Second, women shy away from effective strength training in fear of getting bulky. They are content being weak because they do not know that they can get stronger without developing the bod of a Jesse Ventura. Ladies resort to pathetic high rep programs that do nothing to improve their muscle tone or strength. Indeed, bodybuilding is the worst thing that ever happened to strength training!

If you compare strength training to car racing, conventional bulking up is an unimaginative increase of the engine size. The approach described in *Power to the People!* is radically different. I shall teach you futuristic techniques which will enable you to squeeze more horsepower out of a given size engine. Ladies and athletes from sports where the bodyweight must be kept down, like wrestling and gymnastics, will enjoy a high level of strength without upgrading their clothes' size, and bodybuilders will finally be able to walk the talk with their newly functional muscles.

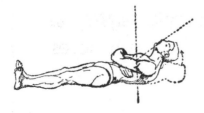

Curl a pencil or your pink Barbie barbell, whichever is heavier. Yeah, I know, the most intense activity you have done since high school is power mousing on your computer. Now curl your vacuum cleaner. Wow! Watch that biceps pop out! Why do your 'pipes' stand out in prominent relief when you are lifting something heavy?—Because tension is the mechanism by which your muscles generate force. Your car's engine blows up a mix of gasoline and air to push its pistons; *Red October's* nuclear reactor boils water and uses the steam to spin a turbine; your muscles tense up.

Tension = Force. The tenser your muscles are, the more strength you display. It is that simple. Watch how the wiry muscles of a kickboxer stand out in sharp relief when a powerful kick makes its impact or how a gymnast's compact deltoids appear rock hard and almost inanimate as he executes a crucifix on the rings.

Force and tension are essentially the same thing. That is why neurological, or 'bulk free', strength training can be summed up as **acquiring the skill to generate more tension.** "Skill is perhaps the most important element in strength," agrees strength researcher from California Prof. Thomas D. Fahey. To acquire that skill—and the super power that comes with it, not to mention the traffic-stopping muscle definition—you must maximize muscular tension in your training. High tension training involves:

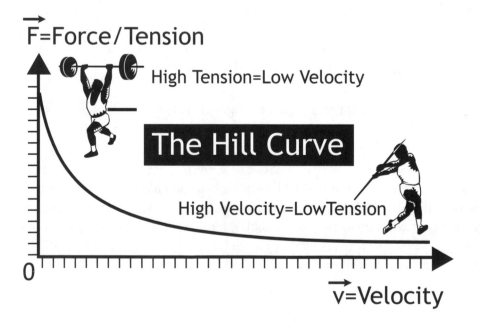

$\vec{F}$=Force/Tension

High Tension=Low Velocity

The Hill Curve

High Velocity=LowTension

$\vec{v}$=Velocity

High tension training has five key conditions:

1) slow exercise performance;
2) maximizing muscular tension, or 'flexing', regardless of the weight used;
3) employing heavy, 85-95% of one's maximum,
   weights at least some of the time;
4) minimizing fatigue;
5) taking advantage of various neurological phenomena.

1) Slow exercise performance

Lifting and lowering your iron slowly is a necessity commanded by your physiology. In the 1920s a scientist named Hill figured out that the force/tension rapidly drops off as the velocity increases:

Muscles cannot give all they have got when they contract fast for various mechanical and neurological reasons. That is why athletes from 'fast' sports have to be content with just a fraction of the strength they are capable of. When you pitch a baseball, you just do not get to push against it long enough to show some real muscle.

Athletes from nearly static sports—powerlifters, arm-wrestlers, and, for a part of their routine, gymnasts—move very slowly and get the luxury of maximally exerting themselves. Watch an arm-wrestling tournament if you get a chance. Two callused hands get locked in a standoff reminiscent of the Cold War. Neither side gives an inch. The velocity is zero and the twenty something muscles of the forearms are outlined like the muscles of a stiff cadaver with its skin removed. No wonder these slow pokes possess spectacular strength and muscle tone, which no other athletes can touch!

2) Maximizing muscular tension, or 'flexing', regardless of the weight used

Tensing your muscles as if you were handling a world record weight, even if you are lifting your grandma's broomstick, teaches you to maximize muscular tension. That, as you recall, is what makes you very strong. Such practice, in part, explains the feats of strength performed by martial arts masters: breaking bricks, absorbing powerful strikes, etc. Karatekas have performed special exercises called *sanchin* which involve maximal dynamic tension of the muscles for centuries.

▼

Karatekas have performed special exercises called *sanchin* which involve maximal dynamic tension of the muscles for centuries.

▲

3) Employing heavy, 85-95% of one's maximum, weights at least some of the time

Then why, you might ask, should I lift heavy weights if I can just pretend with a broomstick or no weight at all, a la the late Charles Atlas?

Three reasons. First, your spine, joints, and tendons must get accustomed to the pressure of 'real' resistance. When a person who has done nothing but dynamic tension exercises attempts to lift a heavy weight, various sensors throughout his body scream to the spinal cord to shut down theoperation because they perceive the load as dangerous. When your muscles shake and then collapse under a barbell that is too heavy, it is the dirty work of these *mechanoreceptors,* the governors of strength. Martial arts masters understood it and complimented their dynamic tension drills with striking hard surfaces and breaking various objects to accustom their bodies to pressure.

And second, most people need the feel of live resistance to get skillful at generating a high degree of muscular tension. Australian exercise physiologists observed that "... the contraction is in fact caused by an electro-chemical signal which the muscle receives IN RESPONSE TO the load..." If you ask a comrade who has not been around iron to contract his internal oblique, for instance, he would not have a clue how to do it, even if you give him an anatomy atlas. Have him perform a Full Contact Twist from my *Beyond Crunches: Hard Science. Hard Abs.* book, and the properly aligned resistance will teach him what to do.

And third is something geeks call the Henneman's size principle. It states that, generally, the heavier is the load you are manhandling, the greater is the muscular recruitment, or tension. In your strength quest there is no way around hoisting some heavy iron at least occasionally.

The mighty Arthur Saxon who performed this stunt regularly when with the circus. The weight of his two brothers shown here was well over 300 pounds. He had no problem bent-pressing them overhead with one arm daily. The 'bent press' is an extreme version of the side press described later in the book. (Photo from Earle Liederman)

4) Minimizing fatigue

High values of fatigue and tension are mutually exclusive. When your muscles, mind, and cardio-respiratory system are tired, you cannot produce much force. Try a heavy bench press after a set of pushups or a five mile run and see what happens! An effective neurological strength program minimizes different types of fatigue by reducing the number of repetitions, increasing the rest periods between the sets, keeping your workout short, and similar measures.

5) Taking advantage of various neurological phenomena

It is an old maxim that in any endeavor the mind holds more potential than any physical transformation. Just watch a wiry old karate master chop a pile of bricks in half, a feat that would send a young bodybuilder to the emergency room. Modern neuroscience offers us a host of very simple techniques that make an immediate positive impact on your strength performance.

All of the above will be explained in detail further in the book. For now, remember that strength is your ability to generate force/tension. **Learn how to tense your muscles harder—and you will get stronger and harder without adding bulk.** Guaranteed.

When it comes to building muscle and might, the gym wisdom is quick to sum it up as the attempt to do another rep when all the reps are done and lift another five pounds when all the pounds are lifted. Sounds cute and macho, like a teenage rock station. It also has as much semblance to reality a that same station's trash morning talk—show.

From Eugene Sandow to Yuri Vlasov, the strongest men and women in the world have never trained to failure! You will not even have to take off your shoes and show your toes to count the exceptions; your fingers will suffice. Cut the 'do or die' rhetoric take a long hard look at yourself, and tell me what are your odds of becoming another exception? If 'training to failure and beyond' is so hot, how come your bench has been stuck at 185 pounds since Arnold's first movie?

Old school lifters maxed or went to failure VERY infrequently. Quoting Earle Liederman in his 1925 classic *Secrets of Strength,* a strong man "never extended himself unless it was absolutely necessary. Once in awhile he would cut loose. It might be against a particularly strong competitor, or just with the desire to see whether he could improve his record." The top power dogs of today follow the same time tested strategy. Ed Coan squats 875x3 and calls it a day although he knows that he could have fived that weight. Heavy training not to failure sure worked for Coan who has set nearly eighty world records.

To understand how a man can squat 1,000 pounds without training to his limit, you have to understand the concept of intensity. It is generally agreed that intensity is the single most important factor in strength training. Arthur Jones, the Nautilus guru, defined it as 'the percentage of the momentary ability', or what you have done compared to what you could have done. For instance, if you curled 100x10 and that was your true limit, you performed with 100% intensity. If you only did 100x5, your intensity would rate a lowly 50%.

According to the 'high intensity training' advocates, or 'HIT Jedis' as they would become known in the *Star Wars* era, the amount of weight you are using is secondary, but you must go to total failure to get stronger. And if you do not, you are wasting your time. According to these characters, Vlasov's and Coan's method could not possibly work. Jimmy Stewart's character in *Harvey* must have been a HIT spokesman: "I wrestled with reality for thirty five years and I am happy to state that I finally won over it."

It is almost the XXI century and world class athletes and housewives alike should have no patience for unscientific touchy-feely training practices! Enter the only scientific definition of weight training intensity: the percentage of your 1RM, or the heaviest weight you can lift once. In Ed Coan's example his 875x3 squat set rates

> ▼
> **Success begets success and failure begets failure.**
>
> *—Dr. Fred 'Squat' Hatfield*
> ▲

87.5% intensity because his max is 1,000 pounds. If the powerlifting champion ate the wrong kind of mushroom and tried the Nautilus workout, he would squat something like 660x12RM. 'RM' stands for 'rep max', or the heaviest weight one can lift for a given number of reps. In this example Coan's intensity would be only 66%, regardless of the amount of suffering and the fact that he pushed to failure.

The Russian definition of intensity reflects the hard, cold, and knurled reality of the iron game. Research on both sides of what used to be the Iron Curtain clearly points to muscular tension, or weight, rather than fatigue, or reps, as the key that unlocks the strength puzzle (e.g., Roman, 1962; Goldberg et al., 1975; Atha, 1981)! In other words, you must push your limits of weight/tension, and not reps/exhaustion if you want to get stronger. It works. New England powerlifter Kirk Karwoski heeded Coan's wisdom and started racking his squats a rep short of collapse. The result was a 1,003 pound squat and muscular development of a T rex. If you think that only sissies hang up their belts before total muscle failure, I suggest that you volunteer your opinion to temperamental three hundred pound 'Captain Kirk' and see how long you live.

Muscle failure is more than unnecessary—it is counter-productive!

Even if you have no desire to set powerlifting records or outgrow your clothes, does not it make sense to use the most effective strength training method available? Especially since it is a lot less miserable than the 'train for pain' alternative?

Muscle failure is more than unnecessary—it is counterproductive! Neuroscientists have known for half a century that if you stimulate a neural pathway, say the bench press groove, and the outcome is positive, future benching will be easier, thanks to the so-called *Hebbian rule*. The groove has been 'greased'. Next time the same amount of mental effort will result in a heavier bench. This is training to success!

The opposite is also true. If your body fails to perform your brain's command, the groove will get 'rusty'. You are pushing as hard as usual, but the muscles contract weaker then before! To paraphrase powerlifting champ Dr. Terry Todd, if you are training to failure, you are training to fail. HIT Jedis, the Force is clearly not with you.

The most intelligent way to develop strength is to lift much heavier weights than most weekend warriors play with but to terminate your sets before your muscles fail. Doing a triple with a weight that you could have done five reps with is a lot safer and more effective that an all-out set of ten. May the Force be with you!

Arthur Saxon's "theory was that light exercises were only tiring and made him no stronger," *The Strong Men of Old* book by Bob Hoffman explains the training methods of a famous lifter of the turn of the century. "...He would do each stunt only a few times and alternate with brief periods of rest so as to prevent himself from tiring. As a result... his rugged and sinewy physique reflected his great strength, strength the like of which the world has never seen since."

Yes, fatigue and strength/tension are mutually exclusive! Metabolic waste products like lactic acid hamper further powerful contractions. Cardiovascular insufficiency forces you to prematurely terminate your set. Mental fatigue from doing too many reps or sets prevents you from generating required intensity. The 'communication lines' between your brain and your muscles get overworked and no longer conduct your orders effectively.

Here is how you can minimize various types of fatigue and get the most out of your strength training:

1) limit the repetitions to five and fewer;
2) increase the rest intervals between sets to a duration of three to five minutes;
3) limit the number of sets to two;
4) pause and relax between reps;
5) do not practice a lift more than five times a week.

* unless you are trying to build muscle, a point I will elaborate on later

1) Limit the repetitions to no more than five

"This tension [from reps] is lower than that developed when a maximal or a circa-maximal weight is lifted once and different in nature as well," stated top Soviet strength expert Robert Roman in the early sixties, when Russians weightlifters showed the world who ruled once and for all. "Besides, as the result of fatigue, the last reps of a set are performed against a decreased excitation of the nervous system. This impedes the formation of the complex conditioned reflex loops needed for further strength improvement."

Performing more than six reps per set hinders strength development! insists Arkady Vorobyev, another leading Russian sports scientist and a former world champion weightlifter. Limiting your reps to five is even better. Many of the world's strongest and hardest bodies have been molded with five and fewer rep sets. "When I began training," recalls powerlifting great Mike Bridges, "I did many repetitions and sets without too much success. When I stopped working on the reps, I began to increase in strength rapidly. I believe you can cut unnecessary reps and sets, and discover an ability to recover much faster. And, you will make bigger gains."

▼

If after your exercise, your bath and your rub-down, you feel fit to battle for a kingdom, then your schedule is right.

—Earle Liederman, Secrets of Strength, 1925

2) Increase the rest intervals between sets to a duration of three to fiveminutes

Health clubs try to talk you into spending as little as thirty seconds between your sets 'to increase intensity and improve your cardiovascular conditioning'. In reality, they want to get you out faster so they can recruit more members and make more money. Soviet exercise physiologist Leonid Matveyev who does not own health spa chain stock recommends three to five minute breaks between sets if one is training the nervous system rather than building muscle.

3) Limit the number of sets

Even if you keep your reps down and rest for a long time between sets, cumulative fatigue eventually sets in. Muscle growth will be stimulated, which is not everyone's objective. That is why the 'strength and tone only' *Power to the People!* workout is limited to only two sets per exercise. One set with the main weight, and one with a 10% lighter barbell. This format is not writ in stone; it just works for most comrades.

4) Pause and relax between reps

It is a standard practice in North America to avoid the locked out position where the joints are supporting the weight. The idea is not to give the muscle any rest and, supposedly, 'save the joints'.

Arthur Jones, the creator of Nautilus, proposed exhausting the muscle as quickly as possible. While it is indeed helpful in building mass, as you will see later in the book, racing the fatigue is counterproductive when steel cable strength and muscle tone are the only objectives.

Pausing and relaxing—as much as safety allows—for a second or so between your reps will not only make you less miserable, but will enable you to generate higher values of muscular tension. As for the bit of advice about not locking out your joints, it is all hogwash. Your joints were meant to lock and support load. In fact, if you do not subject them to stress, you will never be really strong!

It was discovered in the mid-eighties that your knees, elbows, etc. have special mechanoreceptors, or sensors, which respond to loading. If you freak at the thought of putting some weight on your joints, expect your joints to remain weak. Whenever you attempt a heavy lift, the mechanoreceptors will stop your muscles from contracting by sending panic signals to your spinal cord. Old timers understood this well and built what they called 'ligament strength' with various heavy support feats. John Grimek, a legend of American weightlifting and bodybuilding, used to support up to 1,000 pounds overhead! And lived until around ninety years old to tell about it.

▼

If you freak at the thought of putting some weight on your joints, expect your joints to remain weak.

▲

5) Do not practice a lift more than five times a week.

Forget the myth that 'it takes a muscle forty eight to ninety six hours to recover and get stronger'! It does only if your training is not well thought through. "The general idea in planning strength training sessions is to have the athlete do as much work as possible while being as fresh as possible", revealed former consultant to Soviet Olympic teams Prof. Vladimir Zatsiorsky after he jump shipped to the US. Elite Russian and Bulgarian weightlifters have up to twenty-eight sessions a week. "I'm a weightlifter," said world champion Ivan Chakarov from Bulgaria in an interview, "I train six or seven days a week, eight hours a day. I work for the government. When I can't produce, I lose my job."

And if you train like Chakarov, you will lose yours! Most adults who have more than their hair to worry about would do well emulating the power schedule of wiry farmer Bob Peoples whose deadlift record was untouchable for decades by men of any size, although Bob himself did not even weigh a buck eighty! "The number of times per week varied," wrote Peoples in *Developing Physical Strength*, his old fashioned manual which offered a lot more sound advice than most modern books. "More often I trained on average of four to five times a week, but have trained on Monday, Wednesday, and Friday, or every other day. I have also made good progress on one or two days per week. However, I did not follow a one or two day per week pattern very often."

▼

A German study performed in the early sixties discovered that taking more than a day off between strength training sessions reduced their effectiveness by a whopping 50%!

▲

The mighty Arthur Saxon performing his official world's record lift of 448 pounds in the two hand anyhow. (Photo from Earle Liederman)

Peoples' schedule is the ultimate in flexibility. Do your concentrated *Power to the People!* Workout—twenty minutes at the gym at the most!—Monday through Friday, and whenever your life is in a crunch, cut back. You can also take an extra day off from one or both lifts if you do not feel recovered for whatever reason. Just do not use this as an excuse to fall into a regular pattern of once or twice a week training. A German study performed in the early sixties discovered that taking more than a day off between strength training sessions reduced their effectiveness by a whopping 50%! I will elaborate on the scientific reasons for such unorthodox training frequency in a future book. For now, the blind faith of a good Communist will do. Remember, the Party is always right!

Wimps like squawking about the exaggerated 'dangers' of low repetition heavy training and love pitching a high rep Barbie and Ken workout as the 'safe alternative'.

Wrong. Heavy low rep training is the safest way to lift. No, I have not been hit on the head a few times too many in the Soviet military. I will give you at least three reasons why heavy training with up to five reps is much safer than lifting a light weight many times.

First, the stabilizing muscles are prematurely fatigued during high-rep sets—anything over five in my book. Take the squat (please!). Although your legs are doing the job of hoisting the load, your back muscles have to work full time to stabilize the spine in a proper alignment. Your quads, glutes and hammies get to contract and relax like pistons and thus pump fresh blood through themselves. Your lower back, on the other hand, stays locked from the first to the last rep and will unavoidably die first. Once your back gives out—you are toast! One strength training authority who crusades for fifteen to fifty rep squats and deadlifts as a 'safer' form of training has a list of injuries worthy of a Purple Heart: torn knee menisci, multiple pec tears, rotator cuff tears, an arm fracture...

Edward Aston was a famous British middle-weight lifter who bent-pressed over 300 pounds, one hand overhead. (Photo from Earle Liederman)

Contrary to what the public thinks, "Most serious injuries occur during... fatigued states, and from moving out of position, and not during maximum (1RM) attempts," as top US strength experts, Drs. Stone and O'Bryant, like to point out. Powerlifters have a saying that 'five is the most reps God intended for a powerlifter to do'. Not because, as one smart aleck said, they cannot count higher than five. Because with the monster loads they are handling they have a very narrow margin for error and are forced to do everything they can to maximize safety. Dr. Joseph Horrigan who has treated many sports injuries in the Los Angeles area observed that bodybuilders—who generally train to failure—suffer from a lot more pec tears than powerlifters, although the latter bench a lot heavier.

▼

**Don't try
to confuse me
with the facts!**

*—Phil Hartman's
character,*
News Radio
TV show

▲

If you take the hint and do no more than five reps, the involved muscles get fatigued at about the same rate. When the set takes only fifteen to twenty seconds to complete, you are forced to rack the weight for reasons other than compromised circulation. In the example of the squat your back and other stabilizing muscles will not bail out on you just when you needed them most.

The second reason for the superior safety of low rep heavy training is concentration. When you do something five versus twenty five times it is a lot easier to keep your mind on the task at hand. Besides, heavy weights command high respect while light ones do not.

Third, lifting heavy weights allows you to develop awesome strength without training to failure. I have explained this point in the last chapter. You must agree that taking a weight that you could lift six times the 'six rep max', or 6RM and lifting it only five times is a lot safer than cranking out ten reps with a 10RM load!

A better quality of life delivered by low rep weight training is nothing to sniff at either. "I do three sets of ten to twenty reps on all of my exercises," a martial artist asked me once in a magazine, "and I get so sore and tired, that I have no energy left for my martial arts practice!" No wonder. It is well documented in the former Soviet Union by Roman and other scientists that repetitions in excess of five, and especially ten, make one a lot more sore and systemically fatigued than three to five rep sets.

Heavy training, if not overdone, even energizes you! Low rep heavy work, for example three sets of three reps at ninety percent of the athlete's maximum (3x3@90%1RM), is often employed by Russian coaches to produce a tonic effect on their athletes' nervous systems. You can see why the old time strongman said that after a good workout he felt 'ready to battle for a kingdom'!

When you do something five versus twenty five times it is a lot easier to keep your mind on the task at hand.

You have tried high reps. You went for the 'burn'. It did not work. Why do you insist on doing the same thing and expect a different outcome?

The 'burn' you feel from high reps is from lactic acid buildup and does absolutely nothing for toning up your muscles. Pick up a copy of *The Guinness Book of World Records* and look up the picture of 'Captain America' who holds the world record in the number of consecutive sit-ups—in the ballpark of 25,000! This dude must have 'felt the burn' more than anyone else on this planet and he does not even have a six-pack to show for it, even at his low level of body fat.

The reason you feel hard during and after the 'burn' is the same reason a corpse is stiff. Your muscle fibers are like mouse traps—they go off by themselves, but need energy to be reset to contract again. A dead body is out of ATP, the energy compound that relaxes the muscles. A 'stiff's' muscles are permanently contracted. A high rep workout exhausts ATP in your muscle and leads to a temporary hardness very similar to the more permanent rigor mortis! The only way to make such 'tone' last is by killing yourself.

Then what is 'real' muscle tone and how do you get it? Flex your biceps the way kids do when they show off. Wow, the little ball is just rippling under the skin! If you just could walk around flexed like this... you would also develop a taste for canary yellow striped tights and tank tops three sizes too small for you and become a bodybuilder!

If you do not feel like walking around all day feeling and looking constipated, you could just train your nervous system to keep your muscles half flexed when you are relaxed. After all, this is what **muscle tone is—residual tension in a relaxed muscle!** The kind of tension that comes from neurological activity, and not energy exhaustion.

Increased muscle tone is not a physical transformation of your muscle. It is the result of the nervous system being more alert. It keeps the muscles partially contracted all the time so you are more ready for wrestling bears, crushing rocks in a labor camp in Siberia, and doing other useful things for the glory of the Party and the People. When a Russian paratrooper is braced for a kick in the gut from his drill sergeant, he has got the tone!

Strength = tension = tone. It is that simple. Provided you gain strength learning to generate tension, rather than by building muscle, generally the stronger you are, the harder you will be! Strength and tone training is the same thing.

▼

You like burn? Light a match.

—Fred Hatfield, Ph.D., Powerlifting World Record Holder

▲

"Why am I having trouble getting 'the buns of steel'?" wonder millions of ladies. Because the glutes have tremendous strength and leverage. When you see a power-lifter squat or deadlift bar-bending weight, the glutes carry the brunt of that multi-hundred pound load! When you do butt squeezes, 'fire hydrants', or similar silly moves popular in 'muscle sculpting' classes, you do not even come close to tapping the force/tension potential of your body's strongest muscles. You'd better get on a first name basis with heavy deads if you are after a hard butt!

"Why can't I define my triceps to save my life?" wonder men and women alike. An obscure study done in the early sixties discovered that although the triceps is a 'three-headed' muscle, its medial head performs the brunt of the work. The other two heads, the long and the lateral, kick in only when the resistance is very high. According to Dr. Thomas McLaughlin, a biomechanics researcher and a nationally ranked powerlifter, even some powerlifters do not approach the weights needed to recruit the two lazy triceps heads in their training! The most visible part of your triceps is the lateral head on the outside of your arm. It is one of the 'bum' pair and it will remain forever flat and saggy if you keep lifting Ken and Barbie weights!

You want to be ripped? Train heavy! "Then why are bodybuilders more 'cut' than powerlifters?" you might ask. They train with lighter weights than power-lifters, yet they look more defined. Are we missing something?

No. The public stereotype of a weightlifter or powerlifter is that of a three hundred pounder with a beer gut. The lifters in the unlimited class indeed fit this image because they benefit from the extra weight, even fat. It is much easier to come out of a squat if you have a huge belly and thick calves to bounce off! So these men's rock hard muscles are buried under slabs of fat.

Lighter lifters, on the other hand, tend to be very lean to make the most efficient use of the weight allowed by their class. Check out the anatomy chart physique of 198 pound Russian Olympic weightlifting legend David Rigert, the hard body of a petite 123 pound Mary Jeffrey who bench pressed a whopping world record of 275 pounds, or the sinews of John Inzer, a 165 pound Texan with a 780 pound world record deadlift. Ironically, these athletes' looks are the side effect, rather than the result, of their training.

When it comes to bodybuilders, also keep in mind that there is a big difference between looking good without trying, and getting photographed when you are almost bursting from flexing. And don't forget the shave, the oil, the pump, plus expert lighting and photography which could make Woody Allen look almost like a man. And how about amphetamines, thyroid hormones, diuretics, and the kitchen sink bodybuilders take to get 'cut'?

No, the call to heavy metal is not a Communist plot to get all Americans bulky and create a food shortage. Surprise: lifting heavy weights is will not necessarily build big muscles!

When comrades see three hundred pound men five feet tall and four feet wide in strongman contests they confuse the cause and the effect. These guys naturally gravitated towards the iron game because of the leverage advantage they got in the genetic sweepstakes. They lift heavy because they are built that way, not the other way around. Quoting Mark Twain, "Get your facts first, and then you can distort them as much as you please."

What does make your biceps grow? According to the *energetic theory*, a muscle cell possesses a limited amount of energy, or ATP, at any given moment. It is spent two ways: protein synthesis and mechanical work. Normally, a muscle is in an anabolic/catabolic balance. It resembles a pool with the 'in' and 'out' pipes of the same size. Whatever proteins are degraded by your lame daily activities get replaced. However, when a muscle is forced to contract against great resistance AND perform a large amount of work, it uses most of its available ATP supply. Consequently, less energy can be spent on protein re-synthesis. The catabolic processes start prevailing and the muscle mass is reduced.

In the aftermath of this destruction the muscle cell gets a chance to channel its energy to anabolism. It just goes nuts and synthesizes more protein than you had before the workout! Just in case, for the rainy day.

▼

...occasional heavy lifting tends rather to harden the muscle than to rapidly increase its size, protracted effort at lighter but good-sized weights doing the latter to better advantage.

—*William Blaikie,* How to Get Strong and How to Stay So, *1879*

▲

Now, have you figured out yet how to lift heavy without bulking up? Class, anyone? Anyone? I feel like the social science teacher from *Ferris Bueller's Day Off*. If you have not seen this great American classic, I highly recommend it. The teacher is explaining the revenue curve to a class of spaced out drooling kids. Class, anyone knows what 'voodoo economics' is? Or how to get stronger and harder without getting bigger? **Train heavy, but keep the volume, or the total number of reps per workout, low.** The idea is to minimize the amount of 'torn down' muscle—and the reconstruction that follows.

How low is 'low'? The exact number will vary from victim to victim (a kind name for the people I have strength trained), but generally if you keep your reps to ten and under you are in the clear. There are exceptions, of course. Some alien life forms grow like weeds from one heavy set of five reps. If you are one of them, you probably ran away with the circus years ago and will not be reading this book. For the rest of you, Commies, two sets of five is what Lenin ordered for wiry strength.

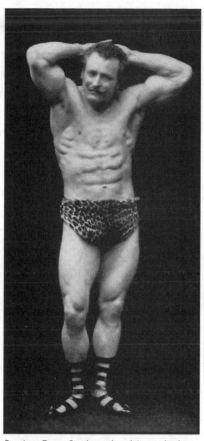

Russian, Eugen Sandow—the ultimate body proportions for all time. Sandow displayed perfect curves no matter how he stood. Even when relaxed, Sandow's abdominal wall was a six pack modern gym rats would envy, (Photo from Earle Liederman)

▼

To get strong and hard without getting big—train heavy but do not do many sets. Thus spake Comrade Stalin.

▲

"No Bulk Here, Comrades!"

If you have been inactive in your former life, any activity, heavy lifting, or even light typing, is likely to add a little muscle to your carcass initially. Do not think of it as new muscle gain, but rather getting back the meat you were supposed to have in the first place. Kind of like after being in a cast or bedridden for years. Most likely your measurements will not increase, while your weight will go up a few pounds. The packing density of your muscles' contractile proteins has increased, the first thing to happen when 'real' muscle growth takes place. Be happy: a denser muscle is a harder muscle.

Keep your sessions brief and heavy if skinny power is what you are after. My friend Dr. Judd Biasiotto squatted an out-of-this-world 605 pounds at an efficient 132 pounds of bodyweight when he trained with a couple of heavy 'triples', as sets of three reps are known in the iron world. Years later Judd became a highly successful master bodybuilder when he upped his volume and started squatting 325x30. His thighs are huge compared to the 'pair of pliers in shorts' that set four world records, yet he is training with half the weight he used to lift. So much for the mainstream bulking up theories.

To get strong and hard without getting big–train heavy but do not do many sets. Thus spake Comrade Stalin.

I owe the title of this chapter to Mauro Di Pasquale, M.D., North American Powerlifting Champion and one of the most knowledgeable comrades on strength training on this continent.

Machine training is often hyped as the thing to do for beginners because free weights are harder to control. "Contrary to common belief," state Prof. Verkhoshansky and Dr. Siff, "*the novice must be taught from a base of mobility to progress to stability,* just as an infant learns to stand by first moving, staggering and exploring the environment."

▼

... check out the weight facility. If there are more machines than weights and you're not in the snack room, think twice before entering.

—Louie Simmons, powerlifting coach extraordinaire

▲

It is best to learn to use free weights when you have the least strength to hurt yourself. Would you rather 'stagger and explore' with fifty or three hundred fifty pounds in your hands? I rest my case.

Paul Chek, an innovative corrective and sports performance exercise specialist from La Jolla, California, proposed an interesting experiment to illustrate this point. Do a set of dumbell bench presses to limit. Without a break continue bench pressing with a barbell loaded with the exactly the same weight as the two dumb-bells you have just used. Once again, go to limit. Next, run over to the Smith machine—a type of an exercise machine with a real barbell in its tracks—loaded with the same weight. You will still be able to lift the weight you have failed with twice!

When you use dumbbells, you control the weight in 3-D. The barbell eliminates one degree of freedom: you cannot move your hands in or out on the bar until you let go of the weight. A machine restricts you to one plane of movement. Your stabilizing muscles get no workout because the machine is doing their job. When you get back to the real world where you have to control your weights, you will expose yourself to an injury in the planes of movement you have not strengthened. Besides, you will not be able to use most of your strength. Your nervous system will shove a brick under your gas pedal when it realizes that the stabilizing muscles are not up to the job. Using the strength built on an exercise machine is like shooting a cannon from a canoe!

In addition to the acute injuries you are asking for if you try to test your machine-built strength in the field, you will be building up micro-trauma for future problems. "The more fixed the object, the more likely you are to develop a pattern overload," explains Paul Chek. "Training in a fixed pathway repetitively loads the same muscles, tendons, ligaments, and joints in the same pattern, encouraging micro-trauma which eventually leads to injury." Compound that risk with the difficulty of lining up your joints with the machine's axis. Machines were built for an 'average person'—and I am yet to meet one.

"Machines are the wusses' way out!"

In the Soviet nation's single-minded drive to succeed in the Olympics, no effort or expense was spared to advance sports science. Yet the Russkies' training facilities look like a junk yard, with plenty of ugly barbells, intimidatingly big plates, and not much else. The evil ones know that free weights are the most natural, versatile, safest, effective, and efficient training tool. Do you?

Strength training expert Dr. Ken Leistner once observed that a body molded with a number of isolation exercises like leg extensions or triceps kickbacks looked like 'a collection of bodyparts'.

Even if you favor the Frankenstein look, you should avoid one-joint exercises. They are inefficient, they negatively affect your athletic performance, and make you more injury prone.

Movements that involve more than one joint form a *kinetic chain*. It is a natural way for your body to perform. When you push your car out of a ditch you do not try to isolate your quads and limit the movement to your knee joint. No, your quads, hamstrings, glutes, and calves work as a team and many joints are involved: the ankles, the knees, and the hips.

Your nervous system develops coordination to manage that team of muscles. This inter-muscular coordination is one of the main factors determining how strong you are when you lift a barbell or move your refrigerator. "How can anyone expect to possess co-ordination in active work when his muscles have never worked together in groups?" asks incredulous Earle Liederman in his 1924 book *Muscle Building*.

Deadlifts, presses, and other full body exercises have inter-muscular coordination very similar to that of the sports you play or the things you do in everyday life. That is why it said that these exercises develop 'functional strength'. Add a few pounds to your deadlift, and you will run faster, jump higher, and get that water softener bag out of the trunk of your car with less effort.

▼

In America convenience was a substitute for power, and comfort the substitute for status.

—*Tom Clancy,*
Executive Orders

▲

In contrast, one-joint drills develop useless strength. In a knee extension strength test conducted at the Ohio State University three world class squatters, including one world record holder, showed a very modest 180 pounds of force, while one mediocre powerlifter broke the Cybex machine! One-joint strength just does not carry over to reality.

Prof. Fahey concludes, "One-joint exercises, such as leg extensions and leg curls, develop movement patterns that will interfere with patterns you use in your sport. Such exercises lead to inappropriate muscle recruitment patterns that can impair movement and lead to injury."

When everything is said and done, muscle isolation is impossible with any meaningful load anyway, as you will learn in the next chapter. So why even bother trying?

Tight!   Tighter!   TIGHTER!

Tension—or weight—is the name of the game. The more you produce, the stronger and harder you will get! Make a tight fist. Where do you feel the tension? Your forearm and biceps, right? Even tighter! White knuckles! Do you feel your shoulder and even chest flexing too?

Like a stone dropped in the water sends ripples across the surface, tension spreads—irradiates—from the muscle directly responsible for the job at hand towards others.

Technically, only the finger flexor muscles in the forearm make a fist. In reality, when the demand for force increases, other muscles jump in on the action. Like a stone dropped in the water sends ripples across the surface, tension spreads—irradiates—from the muscle directly responsible for the job at hand towards others. The bigger the stone, the taller are the waves and the further they spread!

Russians have never been averse to applying solid foreign research to their training. Take the *Sherrington Laws* postulated by one of your countrymen named—surprise! —Sherrington decades ago. One of these 'lieuez', as Chief Inspector Clouseau would say, is the *Law of Irradiation*. It states that a muscle working hard recruits the neighborhood muscles, and if they are already a part of the action, it amplifies their strength! Not by cheating, as some complement their barbell curls with a back swing, but by 'cheering'. The neural impulses emitted by the contracting muscle reach other muscles and 'turn them on' as electric current starts a motor.

Irradiation is one reason compound exercises like bench presses are more effective strength builders than isolation moves like triceps pushdowns. Soviet clinical studies determined that, indeed, strength and endurance of individual arm muscles increased considerably when other muscles were included. I am not talking about the obvious fact that many muscles produce more force than one (duh!). I mean the biceps itself is pulling harder when the neighbors are pulling with it. "...with muscles, as with everything else, "In union there is strength," as Earle Liederman put it.

Thanks to irradiation, we can design a superior efficiency strength workout. If you

Soviet clinical studies determined that, indeed, strength and endurance of individual arm muscles increased considerably when other muscles were included. Here a short lightweight bar is used.

Here a heavier and longer bar is used forcing greater challenges that call on neighboring muscles. I am not talking about the obvious fact that many muscles produce more force than one. I mean the biceps itself is pulling harder when the neighbors are pulling with it.

make a point of lifting respectable weights in exercises like the deadlift, which requires you to pick up a barbell off the floor until you stand erect and lends itself to huge weights, you will start a chain reaction which brings every muscle in your body into play!

"If you could see a photograph of an athlete lifting... in this manner," writes old time physical education director Earle Liederman about a deadlifter, "you would notice muscles sticking out all over him... The forearm muscles naturally stand out in cords and bands, for it takes great gripping power to keep the fingers clenched... The upper-arm muscles stand out, not under lifting strain, but the *holding* strain... The muscles along the full length of the spine also stand out prominently, not because they do much of the lifting, but because they have to keep the body upright. The muscles which stand out most prominently of all are the ones which are doing the actual lifting; namely, the thighs and shoulder-muscles."

Call me biased, but the deadlift is THE exercise of choice for anyone, from a

In a proper deadlift, the forearm muscles naturally stand out in cords and bands, for it takes great gripping power to keep the fingers clenched.
The upper-arm muscles stand out, not under lifting strain, but the *holding* strain

▼
Anyone can relate to bending over and picking up a weight. 'Dip, grip, and rip' is the most normal and common movement.
▲

computer geek to an Olympic athlete! It lends itself to tremendous weights, it teaches you some useful habits for everyday life, and does not require any equipment except a barbell which will not set you back more than $150. At least until you pull over three hundred pounds.

Hardcore metal heads usually praise the squat as the numero uno exercise and 'the measure of a man' (even if you are a woman). I disagree. The squat is a very technical lift. A beginner needs a few months of instruction by a powerlifter before he can do a decent squat. 99% of the squats I have witnessed at health clubs, even by seasoned gym rats, were atrocious in form. Besides, you need reliable spotters and/or a safety rack unless you want to get squashed like a bug if you make a wrong move. The deadlift can simply be dropped which makes it a lot more user friendly. And the deadlift works a lot more muscles than the squat because you must hold on to the bar instead of letting it ride on your shoulders. Any way you look at it the deadlift wins hands down!

For the record, there is a reason why big guys are usually so partial to squats. Comrades who gravitate to serious iron games often have big muscles, short legs, and a long torso. These characteristics give them an advantage in the squat while making the deadlift very difficult. It is not uncommon for a 700 pound squatter to be able to pull but 550 pounds in the deadlift. Partly due to the leverage advantage in the squat and disadvantage in the deadlift, and partly because fancy knee wraps, belts, and canvas suits in powerlifting competitions give a great—100

pounds is not uncommon—boost to one's squat and not nearly as much to the deadlift. Big egos are fragile, therefore the squat in which these guys are good at becomes THE lift.

Let us get real. Anyone can relate to bending over and picking up a weight. 'Dip, grip, and rip' is the most normal and common movement. The squat is a man made game. End of story. Squat fans, please send your hate mail directly to the round file.

"The deadlift is the main exercise," states Igor Sukhotsky, M.Sc., who performs military oriented strength research, "It improves performance in all sports and develops primary power." Sukhotsky knows. This renaissance man used to be a nationally ranked weightlifter and today he competes in full contact karate at fifty something years of age.

While the squat has only been around for a few decades, the deadlift was practiced under different names since the days we stopped walking on all fours. Old timer Earle Liederman recalls his first encounter with this awesome exercise:

"Another man in that gym, who interested me, was an old gentleman who was one of the few amateurs who frequented the place. I did not know his exact age, but from things he said I judged that he was a boy in Civil War days, and must have become interested in exercise in the 1870's; a time at which there was a vogue for a device called a "health-lift". All he was interested in was lifting weights off the floor; and he had made a contraption on which he could load a 100-pound weight and at the top of the affair was a handle, or cross-bar, which reached up about twenty-eight inches. This man had the theory that if every day you thoroughly exercised your back muscles, you would keep your figure, your health, and your strength into advanced old age.

So every afternoon he would drop in and have a short session with his lifting-machine. He would pile on three or four hundred pounds, stand with straight legs, bend his body by arching his spine a trifle, and lift the weight by straightening his back. He would put on more weights and practice what professionals call the "hand-and-thigh lift" [a short range bent knee deadlift—P.T.]. He would keep his back straight and bend his legs at the knees, grasp the handle-bar, so that his knuckles would rest in front of the thigh; and lift the weight by straightening the legs and heaving up the shoulders. After two or three repetitions he would pile more weight, and it was customary to work up to 1,000 or 1,200 pounds [realize that it was a very short movement; the highest weight ever lifted off the floor is 925 pounds—P.T.] before he quit. On one occasion to settle an argument he lifted 1,500 pounds dead weight in the "hand-and-thigh style". I cannot tell you how

This man had the theory that if every day you thoroughly exercised your back muscles, you would keep your figure, your health, and your strength into advanced old age.

▲

long he had exercised in that way, but he must have been at it forty years when I knew him. And as he rarely missed a day, there was a very good reason for his profound faith in his own method of keeping himself strong and healthy."

"One of the factors that makes the deadlift very effective, very hard, and very uncomfortable," writes New York powerlifter and chiropractor Dr. Ken Leistner, "is the fact that it works "a lot" of muscles. One should not think of the deadlift in terms of being a "low back exercise". While the musculature of the low back is certainly involved, that very narrow perspective limits the usefulness and effectiveness of deadlifting consistently. The lift should be initiated by the hips and thighs and finished with the assistance of the low back muscles. Stabilizing the weight and controlling one's body position also calls upon the traps, scapulae retractors, lats, forearms, and hamstrings." Hugh Cassidy, powerlifting world champion of the early seventies, also believed that the deadlift was the best abdominal exercise, bar none. It may make little sense to you right now, but once you work up to an appreciable poundage, you will easily relate to that statement.

There is just one gap the deadlift leaves in your strength: your pressing prowess. "Notwithstanding his ability to lift enormous weights off the ground he could not lift big dumb-bells over head," concludes Liederman in his story of the amazing old gentleman. The pressing musculature just does ,not get enough specific work from deadlifts. Bob Peoples was a farmer from Tennessee who deadlifted 725 pounds, from the floor to lockout—the world record for any weight class before the Great War—at a dainty 178 pounds of bodyweight. Yet Peoples could barely bench press his bodyweight.

So we shall add one pressing movement. I prefer the old fashioned side press over the bench and similar exercises. Consider this the cherry on top of the deadlift to give you complete muscular development. Just remember, as in sales, where 80% of your business comes from 20% of your customers the Pareto Law applies—the press is just a cherry on the top of the deadlift sundae!

Whether you decide to start your workout with the deadlift or the press, is up to you. Many trainers recommend always starting with the exercise which involves more muscle groups, the deadlift in our case. Forget it. For a number of reasons, which I have no desire to dwell on, this generalization does not work as often as it does. Do your own thing. Press-deadlift, or deadlift-press, the Party will let you make one tactical decision on your own.

If you have concerns that muscular imbalance might result with such an abbreviated program, see a chiropractor or a physical therapist—not a personal fitness trainer!—to address them. For most folks it will not be a issue, and for those for whom it is, mindlessly adding more exercises will not fix it. Even the medical community is not clear what the perfect 'balance' is. For example, the widely accepted 3:2 quad to hamstring strength ratio, is pretty much a guess. "...who are we to state what it should be," quips outspoken physiologist Ken Hutchins, "Get both functions as strong as possible and then Mother Nature will decided their proportionality, not us." And, by the way, the deadlift is the best hamstring drill, bar none!

Generally, the higher the weight, the greater the tension. Therefore, **employing exercises which enable us to handle the most amount of weight and then pushing the envelope of resistance in these exercises instead of pushing the reps up will give us the biggest return on our time investment into strength training.** Speaking from experience, the deadlift/press program develops hard and functionally strong bodies! Irradiation with heavy weights and 'big' exercises is the superior and efficient alternative to the Lego method of a million isolation moves.

"With muscles, as with everything else, "In union there is strength"

—Earle Liederman.

"But how can I shape my body with only two exercises?"

Glad you asked. You cannot reshape an individual muscle, even with twenty-two exercises, because of the way your muscles are hooked up to your brain. Each motor nerve, the 'wire' which transmits the commands from your brain to your muscles, controls its own group of muscle fibers called a motor unit. The constituent fibers of a motor unit are evenly spread out throughout the muscle, rather than being concentrated in its 'peak', 'sweep', 'lower', or 'upper' part. Even if you manage to recruit a different motor unit with a different exercise, its fibers will still spin the entire length of the muscle. When a muscle stretches or contracts, it does so throughout its entire length, like a rubber band. The training effect is consistent from one end of the muscle to the other, no matter which end you attach the load to.

Then why do you get sore on one side of a muscle, rather than the other? Probably from tendon inflammation on the loaded end. And burning or tightness during the set is the result of locally restricted circulation. None of the above will reshape your muscles.

A muscle will look different if you build it up, but along the lines of the original shape, like a balloon that you fill up with air. That is why some guy you know built a huge biceps which seems to cross his elbow into his forearm while yours just rolls up your sleeve in a tough little knot whenever you flex it. Your buddy was born with short tendons and long muscle bellies. You, on the other hand, have short muscles and long tendons. When he builds up his bis, the space above the elbow fills up nicely. You cannot do that since your biceps does not extend this far: there is nothing to build in the gap between the muscle and elbow but a ropy tendon.

Naturally, you can go on a selective bodybuilding program. Build up some muscles—not parts of muscles!—more than others, and your body shape will change. If you build the brachialis muscle which lies underneath your biceps, you might get a passable illusion of a bigger 'lower biceps'. I will address these advanced considerations in a future book. For now they would distract you from your mission: the deadlift and the press. It does not do to worry about car polish if your engine and transmission are not up to snuff. I will, however, teach you a very efficient approach to emphasizing various muscle groups which you want to strengthen, tone up, or build up in the context of the Big Two, the deadlift and the press.

▼

If the only tool at your disposal is a hammer, treat everything like a nail.

—Russian saying

▲

Tweak the basic drill to shift a lion's share of the load to your problem area. For instance, switching to a wide, or 'sumo' stance in your deadlifts will give special attention to your glutes. You are specializing on your weakness while still working the rest of your muscles adequately with the same exercise!

In spite of your apparent 'imbalances', chances are that you do not need a specialization program. Build up to respectable poundage on your basic lifts—and the lazy muscles will be forced to do their part!

▼

It does not do to worry about car polish if your engine and transmission are not up to snuff.

▲

What is an Afghanistan-scarred commander of a Russian special forces unit to do when a locust of an inspector descends from HQ? A big wig who joined the military through the Soviet equivalent of ROTC, worked his way up the food chain with intrigue, and never tasted the sweat and blood of the war trade? The general expects Arnold clones performing *Matrix* style acrobatic shootouts. The officer in charge would have as much luck convincing the moron that this is not what the special ops are about as Dilbert would trying to talk his boss out of painting a database blue. So he does exactly what every other Russian professional under incompetent management has been doing since the days of Catherine the Great. Build a 'Potemkin village'.

In the eighties, when the Soviet Empire still had an iron grip on its colonies, it deployed a paratroop division in the Lithuanian city of Kaunas. Its commanding officer developed multiple personalities to do his job right and to keep HQ happy. He organized a 'Hollywood unit' which was busy pumping iron, practicing spinning jump kicks, and leaping over moving vehicles—with the help of an expertly camouflaged trampoline—while shooting up the bad guys.

These guys were awesome! They bulged with muscle and thought nothing of having a stack of bricks smashed on their armored abs with a sledgehammer, shattering a few with nearly any body part, or breaking a thick board struck at them, just by flexing their gorilla traps or shoulders.

I doubt that you are interested in these Russian supermen's acrobatic and martial arts exploits. But I am sure your ears will perk up if I told you that a trooper transferred to a Hollywood unit sported forty-centimeter arms in just a couple of months of training! That is over sixteen inches, Tovarisch!. Get a tape and see for yourself what you would look like when you fill the tape at this mark. What a stud!

A bear of a warrant officer I served with had done a stint with one of those 'Hollywood units' and shared the secret with me. I will send a KGB 'active measures' squad after you if it goes any further!

> ▼
> **It takes a big man to cry, but it takes a bigger man to laugh at that man.**
>
> — *'Deep Thoughts', Saturday Night Live*
> ▲

The premise behind the Russian commando muscle building workout was elegantly simple, as all solid science is. Tension increases the uptake of amino acids, protein building blocks, by the muscles. Therefore the higher is the tension (weight) and the longer time the muscle spends under it (reps)–the better are your chances of making it big. It is like throwing a scoop of protein into your muscles with every rep. The bigger the scoop and the more scoops you have thrown down the hatch—the greater the results.

The logical way to meet the above requirements is to:

1) reduce the reps to 4-6 per set to allow for heavy weights;
2) perform many, 10-20 on average, sets;
3) terminate all the sets a couple of reps before failure to avoid premature fatigue which would force the reduction in weights or/and sets.

The basic *Power to the People!* program which develops strength without bulk calls for one heavy set of five reps and one set with 90% of that weight, for example 100x5, 90x5. A little comrade who wants to become the Big Brother should not stop there. Reduce the weight to 80% of the first 'money' set, and keep doing sets of five reps with short, 30-90sec, rest periods. When you have had enough, that is you cannot lift 80x5 in good form, call it a day. It might take five or twenty five sets, everyone is different. Just do not call it quits too soon. The beefy commando who shared this program with me lifted 40-50 tons every workout. He had to if he wanted to remain a bear.

Weight and rest reduction in the above routine are compromises. Taking a couple of plates off your barbell is necessary to enable you to do multiple sets. A reasonable compression of the rest intervals promotes growth hormone production. HGH, like muscular tension, increases amino acid uptake by the muscles; read: builds them. Less rest between sets also enables you to squeeze your workout into forty-five minutes, supposedly the top end limit for optimal testosterone release.

Because of the increased work load you may have to reduce your training frequency somewhat, but restrain yourself from cutting back too much. The US powerlifting community used to accept training each lift once a week and keeping their set number low as the gospel. Recently it has been raving about a multiple set, low rep, three-sessions-for-each-lift-per-week workout, imported from Germany by Stephan Korte. Heavy but never-to-failure, frequent, and high volume training delivers!

▼
The beefy commando who shared this program with me lifted 40-50 tons every workout.
He had to if he wanted to remain a bear.
▲

Which exercises should you do with your commando muscle program? Deadlifts, perhaps? Good guess!

"His thighs, both back and front, were unusually big and his calves were enormous," awed Liederman describes a physique built with nothing but deadlifts. "Naturally he had big chains of muscles along the spine, but the striking thing was the phenomenal development of the trapezius muscles, which are in the upper back just below the base of the neck. These muscles, when they contract, "shrug up' the shoulders, and when he did his "hand-and-thigh" lift and heaved his shoulders up, you could see these muscles bunch themselves into enormous masses. Even when standing at ease these muscles were so big that they made his shoulders slope at a high angle from the deltoids to the sides of his neck. No ready-made coat would fit him. His forearms—especially the outside parts of them—were covered with muscles so powerfully developed that there were big furrows between them. His grip was something to be avoided. His biceps muscles were pronounced in their size..."

Life is too short to be small.

—Benjamin Disraeli

Yes, you can build huge muscles on a super abbreviated program of deads and presses! There is no need to do other drills. "If you work the heck out of the deadlift," Mr. America Tony Pandolfo used to say in his heyday in the sixties, "you'll get growth in your upper and lower back, thighs, and hips. If you press or bench hard, your upper body will take off." Words to live by.

William Gerardi—A turn of the century athlete whose 31 inch thighs are rare for a period that preceeded the age of squat obsession.

Having done your job as a human crane, go home and eat. A lot. I am not going to waste my time taking apart the incompetent studies by pencilnecks that 'prove' that you do not need any extra protein to build muscle. Russian research is clear: you do, and a lot of it. Meat, eggs, milk—whatever works for you. How much is an individual matter; experiment. Do not buy into the third grade arithmetic of the simple minds who think along straight lines. In the non-linear Alice's Wonderland of your body a gram of fat may be worth more or less than the accepted nine calories and it takes a lot more that an ounce of protein to build an ounce of

muscle. I may elaborate on this point and other implications of the complexity theory on your training in a future book, for now just remember that the Party is always right!

If having the muscular development of a Calvin Klein model does not satisfy you and you desire to be huge, you could try the following maneuver of Marty Gallagher's prize powerlifting pupil Kirk Karwoski. "I started eating every hour on the hour –high protein..." says this dinosaur, 300 pounds and ripped, "I'd set the alarm twice a night so I could get up and eat. But it paid off."

Is it healthy?—Hell, no. But who ever said that weighing 250 pounds plus was healthy? Muscle, or fat, the extra weight undoubtedly provides extra work for all of your body's systems. Do you prefer a long life or huge muscles? It is America, the land of choices.

Another step to take towards seventeen inch arms is to buy the Anabolic Diet book by Mauro Di Pasquale, M.D. This Canadian doctor and former powerlifting champion's eating plan maximizes your natural production of anabolic hormones by selecting the right foods at the right times. Unlike the typical bodybuilding blah of tuna and rice, Di Pasquale's plan is a feast. To order the *Anabolic Diet,* call (800) 582-2083.

A critical piece of the big biceps puzzle is rest. Old timers used to say, "Don't run if you can walk, don't walk if you can stand, don't stand if you can sit, and if you sat, might as well lie down and take a nap." Cut back on your yard work, add an extra hour or two of sleep every night and an odd nap in between, and in a couple of months DEA agents might knock on your door looking for steroids!

Getting adequate rest also means not being a high strung type. Stress creates a highly catabolic, or muscle destroying, endocrine environment. Learn to relax, take up Chi Kung! Call Dragon Door Publications at (800) 899-5111 and get a free catalog of resources on this fine art of self-improvement. Once you have developed a calm, undisturbed state of mind, your bodybuilding gains will be magnified.

Here you have it. The complete Russian recipe on how to become a bear!

▼
Cut back on your yard work, add an extra hour or two of sleep every night and an odd nap in between, and in a couple of months DEA agents might knock on your door looking for steroids!
▲

Can I get built up with a very light weight by pumping my muscles up?"

Yes, if you are willing to settle for Potemkin village muscles.

"Some years ago a certain Mr. America came to New York to give an exhibition," reminisces professional strong man Sig Klein in his old age. "I always admired his photos and asked him to show me his arm. He refused, saying that he had just made the long flight from California and this could have shrunken his arms. I was flabbergasted. If a few hours trip or a few days layoff from training makes that much difference in his muscles, then those muscles were useless and I didn't care to see them."

Back in the fifties California bodybuilders took up 'muscle spinning', a purely cosmetic activity, like using Rogaine, or getting silicone implants. They would strut around a mirror all day and pump up their biceps with their grandmother's dumbells. Like a leaking tire, the golden boys' muscles had to be daily refilled with blood. It explains the California physique star's unwillingness to show his muscles, deflated after a day's layoff from pumping.

In addition to a long term pump, high rep training leads to 'fake' muscle growth.

There are two types of muscle growth. Myofibrillar hypertrophy, or 'real' muscle growth, is an enlargement of the muscle fiber as it gains more myofibrils, things which contract and generate tension. The muscle gets stronger and harder. Myofibrillar hypertrophy is accomplished by training with heavy weights.

Sarcoplasmic hypertrophy, on the other hand, is a worthless increase in the volume of the muscle cell fluid as a result of high rep training. The fluid, sarcoplasm, accounts for 25-30% of the muscle's size.

Mitochondria, the 'power plants' of the cell, which, when well developed, make up 20-30% of the muscle's size also grow from high reps. The same applies to capillaries: an early eighties study found twice as many capillaries per muscle fiber in elite bodybuilders than in normal subjects!

Needless to say, building things like capillaries or increasing cell fluid volume is form above the function. I have no respect for that.

▼

Physical strength is all very well if one has a purpose for it.

Otherwise it's just a nuisance and a distraction, like wings on a dodo.

—*Robert Sheckley,*
Immortality, Inc.

▲

Myofibrillar Hypertrophy
VS.
Sarcoplasmic Hypertrophy

▼

In addition to a long term pump, high rep training leads to 'fake' muscle growth.

▲

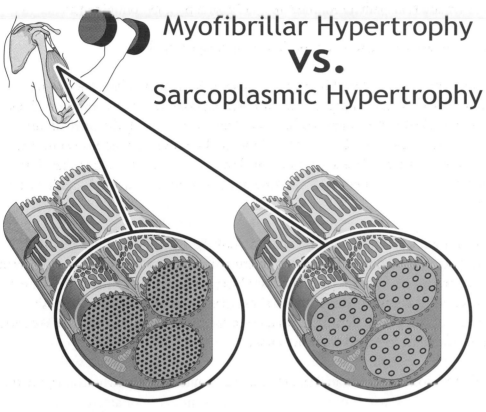

Myofibrillar Hypertrophy
- Denser and stronger muscle

Sarcoplasmic Hypertrophy
- Bloated, soft and useless muscle

"And what about 'muscle confusion'? Just two exercises? Shouldn't I change my program to keep improving?"

Yes and no, a truly Zen answer.

You come into a room and smell something. Pleasant, or unpleasant, it is beside the point After awhile you start screening out the smell, the so-called rebound phenomenon. What would it take to get your nose to react again? Increase the intensity of the smell, or get assaulted by a new flavor.

Your body responds to exercise in the same manner. As former Mr. Universe Mike Mentzer put it, "First we get the swing of things, then we get pretty good at them, but finally we tire of them." After awhile the same old thing has no training effect whatsoever. Your workout has to change if you are to keep making progress. Unfortunately, very few coaches have mastered the black magic of effective exercise variation. Unless you are dealing with postural muscles like the abs, there is a lot more to this voodoo art than switching to another exercise for the given muscle group or isolating the weakness with some other drill. Do not believe your personal trainer with a weekend certification course that triceps pushdowns will help when your bench press has stalled. It may build some new mass, but never strength. Heed the words of G. J. Nathan: "The confidence of amateurs is the envy of professionals."

Russian weightlifting coaches have one hundred and fifty special exercises at their disposal to assure their charges' non-stop progress and sophisticated algorithms that help them employ the right exercises at the right time. This is obviously a 'don't try it at home' method.

If you disregard what I have just said and switch to a different set of exercises every time you hit a plateau, you will fall into the vicious circle described by Ken Hutchins: "A novice usually requires about six weeks to become reasonably confident and competent on a basic... routine of exercises... At about the six-week point, the novice begins to lose his feeling of novelty... It is then that he states that he is bored with his present routine. He requests to learn new exercises. A battery of new exercises, of course, renews his attitude of novelty... At the six-week point, the novice has just obtained an objective base line with his original routine... His instructor assumes the base line... to indicate a performance plateau; so what does he do but recommend a change of routine. This satisfies the subject's whim to see the resistances ever improving again. And to the instructor this confirms his belief that he successfully broke the subject's plateau. In reality, the subject's progress has to start practically from scratch anew. He must go through the process of mastering new exercises... for another several weeks to attain a base line once more."

▼

The height of cultivation runs to simplicity. Half-way cultivation runs to ornamentation.

-Bruce Lee

▲

Today's folks have a short attention span. Ellington Darden, Ph. D. made a good point that most people do not have what it takes to be successful at any endeavor, marriage, studies, or a diet, for more than six weeks. Once you have gotten the basic form down pat, it is time to pick up the stuff that really matters: learn to maximize the tension in the involved musculature and integrate the tension of different muscles into a focused superhuman effort, what karate masters call kime. "If you change the components in training, then you are constantly stiff and you must retrain constantly. What good is that?" exclaims coach Charlie Francis who has kept his notorious charge, Canadian sprinter Ben Johnson, on a steady diet of squats, benches, and a couple of other basics, for years. However the routine's load was varied. That is the approach that you should take. Cycling, or a planned variation of your intensity and volume with the same exercises is explained in the next chapter. Cycling will keep the gains coming without complicating your program. And, because you stick to the same two drills, it will allow you to live relatively free of muscle soreness.

We do not know for sure what causes muscle soreness—don't get me started on lactic acid; it ain't it—but switching to new exercises will make you sore. Be warned that how miserable you feel the morning after is not an indicator of progress! No correlation has been established between getting sore and getting stronger. Some comrades are hurting units for five days following their leg workout yet lift the same weights for years. Others never ache—very annoying, if you ask me—but keep getting stronger from workout to workout.

Never interpret soreness or stiffness as signs of progress. And do not get hung up in variety for variety's sake. Stick to the basics, the deadlift and the press. It is possible to achieve spectacular results with a very abbreviated program, as long as one pays attention to details.

"Keep your program simple. Avoid distractions. Complex programs are wrought with pitfalls and drain the focus. Do only things that help most. Concentrate your energies on doing few tasks well, rather than many tasks poorly." This is the advice of world record bench presser J.M. Blakley.

▼
Never interpret soreness or stiffness as signs of progress. And do not get hung up in variety for variety's sake. Stick to the basics, the deadlift and the press.
▲

Gym rats love reciting the story of Milo of Crotona to illustrate the principle of progressive overload. According to the legend, this ancient Greek started lifting a young calf daily. Milo kept growing stronger and stronger as the animal grew into a bull. From calves to bulls, from bulls to elephants, from elephants to whales. Sure.

"Progressive overloading produces diminishing, and ultimately zero, returns," writes Professor Verkhoshansky, top Russian strength training expert. If you started lifting at the age of sixteen with a 60 kg or 130 pound, bench press, says Verkhoshansky to illustrate his point, and add one kilo, less than 2.5 pounds, per week, you will be lifting 1,275 pounds by the age of twenty six and 2,240 pounds by the time you are thirty six years old! Yeah, right. Dream on.

Why can't you train heavy full time and progress indefinitely? No-one knows for sure. But we are certain that if you try you will only go backwards. "A prize-fighter preparing for an important contest will spend six weeks in training for the battle," noted US physical education director Earle Liederman in the beginning of the century. "Experience has shown that an athletic man can be brought to the very top notch condition in that length of time. And if the training is too prolonged, the athlete will become over-trained or "stale" and will lose energy."

When Stalin was still around Soviet scientists observed that in order to reach top form, an athlete must exhaust his adaptivity, or the ability to improve, greatly. That meant the peak had to be followed by an unavoidable drop in performance. A decade later, in Khruschev's times, Russian researcher Leonid Matveyev analyzed a great many athletes' training logs and concluded that things worked out a lot better if the athlete voluntarily backed off after a push instead of carrying on at full throttle and waiting for a crash. "...continuing training with high loads unduly magnifies the drop in performance while reduced training helps overcome the decrease in performance and ensures a new improvement," as another big brain from the former Soviet Union, Estonian Dr. Atko Viru, summed up this idea.

"Literally he has worked himself out,'" writes strongman Earle Liederman three quarters of a century ago describing a man of iron who has the habit of regularly pushing the envelope, "and this is exactly the thing the strength-seeker cannot afford to do." The guy's name must have been Milo. Matveyev would have told the ancient Greek who had maxed out with his bull to start over with another calf! Taking a step back after you have taken two steps forward is the essence of his periodization or cycling approach to strength training which revolutionized the strength world.

▼

Catch the wave, and you'll be on top of the world!

—The Beach Boys

▲

Cycling enables even world class athletes to improve year after year, when progress would have come to a screeching halt if any other strength training method was used! "Periodization is the best way to train... There were guys around who worked to their limit either on reps or singles all the time in their training, but they didn't last long," recalls Terry Todd, Ph.D., one of the forefathers of American powerlifting. "They either burned out or got an injury of some sort. Those of us who lasted and continued to improve found that we had to start out conservatively—to use light weights for a while and then go on to the increasingly heavier poundage. Then, following a meet, we'd always take a break before coming back to begin again with light weights."

Cycling is about a gradual buildup of intensity to a personal best, and then starting all over with easy workouts. Using the earlier smell analogy, once your nose has stopped responding to the aroma although its intensity has been cranked up, you lower the stimulation, walk out of the room perhaps. Your system will become responsive to the stimulus again. Now it is time to build up to a new peak! A smart powerlifter typically takes a week off after a meet, then he resumes his training with light weights. Some iron heads call this process 'softening up'. Slowly, over a period of eight to sixteen weeks, he builds up the poundage until he peaks with a new personal best. Then he starts all over with a weight slightly heavier than in the beginning of the previous cycle. Like a karate master who has reached greatness in his art and turns in his black belt to wear a beginner's white belt again.

Cycling is the ultimate formula of strength which succeeds where other methods, often a lot more complicated, fail. Do yourself a favor and jump on the bandwagon with the world's strongest people. You will gain beyond your wildest dreams. You will suffer fewer, if any, injuries. Dr. Joseph Horrigan, a Los Angeles chiropractor who fixes up many elite athletes, could not help noticing that those who cycle their lifts experience a lot fewer injuries than those who do not. Powerlifters who have been practicing cycling compete at the international level in their forties and even fifties, while bodybuilders who always push the pedal to the metal burn out, get hurt, and quit at half that age.

Accept the necessity to take a step back in order to take two steps forward. Those who insist on stepping only forward are walking on a treadmill. If hard work was all it took to get strong, there would not be such a thing as sports science. No, pushing the pedal to the metal all the time will get you nowhere fast! And if your head cannot take it and you cannot help pushing your ever-so-stable limits every time you train, see a therapist.

Here is a couple of powerlifting cycles for you to choose from which are short, sweet, and do not take an advanced math degree to follow.

Types of Cycles

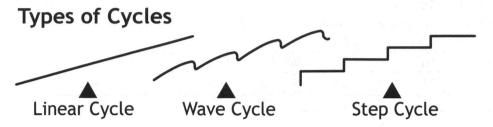

Linear Cycle   Wave Cycle   Step Cycle

The Linear Cycle

Start the cycle with one set of five reps (1x5) with a comfortable weight. 70-80% of your best set of five (80% 5RM) is a good starting place, but you do not need to be so exact. The weight you could easily do ten reps with is about right to start with.

Say you have lifted an empty bar, or 45 pounds, and did five reps. It felt light. You added twenty pounds. Still a feather. 85 and going strong. 95 felt good, but you start noticing it. You decide to add just a little more weight. 100x5 feels just right. You could have done ten reps with this weight, but you know better. Let it be the starting weight for your first power cycle: 100x5.

Rest for a few minutes, and do another set of five reps with 90% of the weight you have just used: 90x5. Do not be pedantic about fractions; round up the numbers. The lighter set is there to double the workload without tiring you out, especially in the end of the cycle when the first set gets downright brutal.

Add five pounds to the first set every workout, and recalibrate the second one accordingly.

Before you know it, things will get heavy. Do not attempt a rep unless you are 100% certain you are going to make it in good form! Just drop the rep or reps that you have not made and carry on the cycle until you are down to two or three reps. Another option is not to peak at all, but terminate a cycle once you have made a little gain, say five pounds per lift, over a previous one.

Cycles vary in length but generally should consist of no fewer than eight workouts. A competitive lifter has to plan his cycle in advance to peak in a competition. You do not need to worry about it. However you should note how well cycles of different lengths work for you and try to plan accordingly.

▼

Cycles vary in length but generally should consist of no fewer than eight workouts.

▲

Here is a hypothetical linear cycle:

Workout Number	1st set Weight	x	reps	2nd set Weight	x	reps
1	100	x	5	90	x	5
2	105	x	5	95	x	5
3	110	x	5	100	x	5
4	115	x	5	105	x	5
5	120	x	5	110	x	5
6	125	x	5	115	x	5
7	130	x	5	115	x	5
8	135	x	5	120	x	5
9	140	x	4	125	x	5
10	145	x	2	130	x	5

You probably could have lifted 150x2 next workout, but you decided to play it conservative and saved it for another cycle. Take a few days off, and start another cycle with a slightly heavier weight then the previous one. It might look like this:

Workout Number	1st set Weight	x	reps	2nd set Weight	x	reps
1	110	x	5	100	x	5
2	115	x	5	105	x	5
3	120	x	5	110	x	5
4	125	x	5	115	x	5
5	130	x	5	115	x	5
6	135	x	5	120	x	5
(135x5 is your old limit.)						
7	140	x	5	125	x	5
8	145	x	5	130	x	5
(145x5RM—your new best set of five a 10 pound gain is awesome!)						
9	150	x	3	135	x	5

The end of cycle. As you see, the cycle started with fairly easy workouts and gained momentum. It kept getting more intense until it culminated in a new personal record. You have added 10 pounds to your best set of five in eight workouts, which may have taken you anywhere from two to nine weeks. A great improvement! Your muscle tone will certainly reflect it.

Understand that results will vary from person to person and from cycle to cycle. While an advanced lifter is content with a five pound gain on his bench press in twelve weeks, a beginner in that period of time may add fifty pounds to his or her dead. The deadlift will always progress faster than the press because your neurological efficiency, or the ability to recruit as much muscle as possible. is higher in your upper body and thus has less room for improvement. Math matters too. Adding 10 pounds to a 200 pound deadlift is only a 5% increase, while it is a whopping 20% for a 50 pound press. One of the implications is that your deadlift cycle might out-run your press cycle. No sweat, treat them as two independent cycles; only competitive lifters have to go to all the trouble of matching them.

There are times when an illness or a trip keeps you away from the gym longer than you wanted. If you have skipped more than a week of lifting, or simply are having a really bad day, back up two or three workouts and resume your cycle. If in the above example you had a two week gap after workout #6, here is what you do:

▼

If you have skipped more than a week of lifting, or simply are having a really bad day, back up two or three workouts and resume your cycle.

▲

Workout Number	1st set Weight	x	reps	2nd set Weight	x	reps
6	135	x	5	20	x	5
a two week vacation in Russia (you are brave!)						
7	125	x	5	115	x	5
8	130	x	5	115	x	5
9	135	x	5	120	x	5
10	140	x	5	125	x	5
11	145	x	5	130	x	5
12	150	x	5	135	x	5
(your new best set of five; a 15 -vs. 10-pound gain!)						
13	155	x	2	140	x	5

Yes, sometimes you will reach a higher peak if you take a step back in the middle of the cycle! Soviet studies determined that such wave cycling—as opposed to the basic linear cycling—is highly effective. Feel free to experiment with these 'cycles inside a cycle' even if you do not have to take training breaks. You could back off here and there when you are having an off day:

The Flexible Wave Cycle

Workout Day	1st set Weight	x	reps	2nd set Weight	x	reps
Mon	200	x	5	180	x	5
Tue	205	x	5	185	x	5
Wed	210	x	5	190	x	5
Thur	200	x	5	180	x	5
	(feeling fatigue from three days of training, decided to back off)					
Fri	205	x	5	185	x	5
Sat	off					
Sun	off					
Mon	210	x	5	190	x	5
Tue	215	x	5	195	x	5
Wed	210	x	5	190	x	5
	—too tired, late night					
Thur	215	x	5	195	x	5
Fri	220	x	5	200	x	5
Sat	off					
Sun	off					
Mon	225	x	5	205	x	5
Tue	230	x	3	205	x	5
Wed	215	x	5	195	x	5
	(you feel that you can hit 230x5 on a second try)					
Thur	220	x	5	200	x	5
Fri	225	x	5	205	x	5
Sat	off					
Sun	off					
Mon	230	x	5	205	x	5
	(you were right, but 230x5 was very exhausting and you take a step back to recover for another push)					
Tue	220	x	5	200	x	5
Wed	225	x	5	205	x	5
Thur	230	x	2	205	x	5
	(you could not repeat your Monday workout; it happens. You have milked this cycle dry. Time to wrap it up.)					

... or follow a more organized approach, for instance four steps forward and three back:

The Structured Wave Cycle

Workout Number	1st set Weight	x	reps	2nd set Weight	x	reps
1	200	x	5	180	x	5
2	205	x	5	185	x	5
3	210	x	5	190	x	5
4	215	x	5	195	x	5
5	205	x	5	185	x	5
6	210	x	5	190	x	5
7	215	x	5	195	x	5
8	220	x	5	200	x	5
9	210	x	5	190	x	5
10	215	x	5	195	x	5
11	220	x	5	200	x	5
12	225	x	3	205	x	5

▼

Because an effective cycle generally lasts between eight and sixteen workouts, five pound jumps each workout would be too much for this trainee.

▲

Because an effective cycle generally lasts between eight and sixteen workouts, five pound jumps each workout would be too much for this trainee. The max will be reached too soon, not allowing one to build enough of what one fellow aptly named 'gaining momentum.' Some people use tiny, one pound and even lighter, plates to solve the problem. Don't bother. Just stay at the same weight for two or even three workouts, then add five pounds. Soviet experience proved step cycling to be a very powerful strength builder. Here is a hypothetical step cycle for someone with a top set of five with 100 pounds (100x5RM):

The Step Cycle

Workout Number	1st set Weight	x	reps	2nd set Weight	x	reps
1	80	x	5	70	x	5
2	80	x	5	70	x	5
3	85	x	5	75	x	5
4	85	x	5	75	x	5
5	90	x	5	80	x	5
6	90	x	5	80	x	5
7	95	x	5	85	x	5
8	95	x	5	85	x	5
9	100	x	5	90	x	5
10	100	x	5	90	x	5
11	100	x	5	90	x	5
12	105	x	5	95	x	5
13	105	x	5	95	x	5
14	110	x	4	100	x	5
15	110	x	5	100	x	5
16	115	x	3	105	x	5

If you wish, you can switch from one basic exercise variation to another—for instance, from conventional to sumo deadlifts—at the beginning of a new cycle. You can also trade one type of a cycle for another, say linear for wave. Other changes are not recommended. You have to follow too many rules to make them right.

Greater strength gains, higher safety, fewer hard workouts... If you have a better deal than cycling, keep your Brooklyn Bridge for yourself!

▼
Greater strength gains, higher safety, fewer hard workouts... If you have a better deal than cycling, keep your Brooklyn Bridge for yourself!
▲

Nature has downloaded a lot of useful software into our nervous systems so we can function efficiently. For example, one neural program, or reflex arc, makes your body follow your head. That is why it is easier—and safer—to deadlift with your head up: the muscles that extend the neck order all the muscles on your backside to contract.

Some of these helpful neural programs are easily run, while others require a little skill to hack into. The next few chapters will teach you how to use various muscle software to maximize your strength training effectiveness and safety. It is almost the XXI century. It's time to learn to use your computer for something other than hammering nails!

Let's start with irradiation. You can milk this phenomenon for all its strength amplifying worth by intentionally bringing even more muscles into play. Simply squeeze the barbell hard on all upper body exercises and flex your abs and glutes on all lifts! Enter hyperirradiation, a high intensity technique that delivers a no delayed gratification strength boost. Powerlifters whom I taught this deceptively simple move report a typical increase of ten pounds on their bench press the first time they try it!

In addition to its powerful force building effects the new 'anti-isolation' technique dramatically increases workout safety by stabilizing the trainee's body and forbidding heaving and bouncing. I suggest that you immediately test the safety and effectiveness of hyperirradiation with barbell or dumbell curls.

First do a few curls in the accepted 'good form', your body upright and no cheating with your back. When things start getting hard simultaneously do the following:

- squeeze the weight as if you are trying to crush it to pulp;
- squeeze your glutes as if pinching a coin with them;
- tighten your abs as if bracing for a punch.

You will have an easier time integrating your abs and glutes into the action if you follow this advice of the late karate great Masatoshi Nakayama: "For strength and stability, it is necessary to have the feeling that the line connecting the navel and the anus is short as possible."

▼

Employing every tooth and claw In the awfullest way you ever saw...

—E. Field

▲

1. The cheat curl — For HMO members only

2. The regular curl— Quite safe, but weak

3. The hyper curl— Heavy and strict. Accept no compromises!

Once you have done the three secret moves, the weight will immediately acquire whimsical lightness. You will be able to crank out a few extra reps—and do it in your best form ever! Your body will freeze in a rock hard position of maximum safety. When the reps get harder, the bell will slow down but will keep moving slowly without any assistance of body English because the body will get even more braced. Talk about safety!

Hyperirradiation—"Cheering", not "Cheating"

1 Brain gives order to "Contract!"

3 Upper body muscles help to "Contract!"

2 Biceps contracts

3 "Core" muscles of abdomen and low back help to "Contract!"

3 Leg muscles help to "Contract!"

You cannot shoot a cannon from a canoe. You cannot lift a respectable weight safely unless your whole body is tightened up and braced against the ground. So many weight training injuries take place when the trainee starts squirming under the load if the latter starts feeling heavy. The brain dead mainstream advice of 'isolating' one muscle at the exclusion of everything else is largely responsible for these injuries. Learn the above 'anti-isolation' technique, stabilize your body by overall muscular tension, and your odds of getting injured will plummet faster than Dow Jones on 'Black Monday'.

Martial arts masters understand how body tension improves one's stability, which is one of the reasons formal exercises like sanchin which require maximal tensing of the whole body are practiced. "Mr. Uechi performed these feats not to show how strong he was but to prove to his students that the human body has not so many limitations as most people believe it to have," tells my time-yellowed book *The Way of Karate*. "He wanted to stress the importance of sanchin by doing feats which he said required no other methods but sanchin.

"The first feat he demonstrated was the stability test. He asked two of his largest and strongest students to pick up a large bamboo pole hanging over the door to his school and place it against his stomach. He then positioned himself in a sanchin stance and requested the two students to push as hard as they could. They did so for a minute or two, but they were unable to budge Mr. Uechi an inch."

Old time Olympic weightlifters, better educated than today's iron heads, understood this concept clearly and braced themselves against the ground before pressing a barbell overhead. "This full tension of the thighs and buttocks is of utmost importance because it provides a solid base for pressing," wrote Englishman George Kirkley, in bold type, in the early sixties. Slack muscles of the body absorb 'the recoil' of the muscles directly responsible for the task at hand and let their strength dissipate in the flesh instead of lifting the weight. Time went by and then men, and later women, took up the habit of exercising lying down—I was surprised when I did not find the bench press in a book named *Exercising in Bed*. The ancient secret of power and stability was lost.

"Keep every body part tight during the entire movement". Powerlifting world champion Ernie Frantz instinctively understood irradiation of tension when he developed this Fifth Commandment of Powerlifting. "As long as your body is tense and rigid, the risk of injury is small," says Iron Ernie. "Picture this: You go to squat, your legs are tight, but your arms are lightly clutching the bar. What will happen is the weight will feel heavy and probably shift on you. Now if you were holding on firmly with every muscle ready for action, you would probably make the lift with ease."

I will sum up the benefits of hyperirradiation, or purposeful tensing of muscles other than the ones directly responsible for the task at hand:

1) increased strength through additional neural stimulation of the target muscles by the impulses from working 'extra' muscles;

2) increased strength through providing a solid and efficiently aligned foundation to lift from ("Give me a pivot point, and I will turn the world upside down!" bragged ancient Greek scientist Pythagoras);

3) improved workout safety through dramatically improved body stability.

Old time Olympic weightlifters, better educated than today's iron heads, understood this concept clearly and braced themselves against the ground before pressing a barbell overhead.

'Surrounding' the working muscle by commands from the center (abs/glutes) and the periphery (hand and forearm muscles) leaves the former no choice but be stronger! When Dr. Ken Leistner of Long Island, NY reached a certain poundage in a deadlift, his grip strength started limiting him and he was tempted to use straps which unload your hands by making the barbell hang off your wrists. But he did not. "When I made the decision to forego the use of straps and persevere until I could handle heavy weights without them, I surpassed my previous bests. In fact, the entire exercise became much more intense and my overall gains in strength and muscular size were quite unexpected. Perhaps my level of concentration was higher because I was so intent on maintaining my grip on the barbell.

As neuroanatomists know, the area of the brain that exerts control over the hand muscles has a much higher representation relative to actual muscle size than other muscle groups. Although it is strictly conjecture, perhaps intense forearm/hand work heightens neural stimulation for all muscles worked during a particular movement. My experience has shown that taking the time and energy to directly stimulate the forearm musculature leads to increased ability to handle heavy weights in many exercises."

Even if you do not bother with squeezing a tennis ball or doing other specialized grip exercises, the hand strengthening effect of your deadlifts, plus concentration on squeezing the life out of your barbell every time you lift it will pay off handsomely with new strength in all your lifts! You will also protect your wrists during your presses. In every gym you see people pressing with their wrists hyperextended, or collapsed back. Not only does this maneuver rob you of your power, it also damages the ligaments and makes you a candidate for carpal tunnel syndrome.

And what about the abs? In a recent poll, nearly an equal number of men and women responded that it is the most important body part to develop. Frequently cosmetic preferences are evolutionary choices we are making without being aware of it. Large widely set eyes are not only attractive but provide their owner with fine stereoscopic vision that may play a role in survival. Heroin-emaciated models have taken over the media but men still prefer women who do not look like adolescent boys. Although perpetuation of his genetic code may be the last thing on a guy's mind, he is attracted to a gal who is most fit to be a mother—which is why she has all the right curves.

Simon Javierto demonstrating the phases of isolation of the abdominal muscles. This control is accomplished by complete exhalation of all air from the lungs drawing in the abdominal wall to fill the vacuum (second photo). Then by bending forward and contracting the rectus abdominus (first photo). (Photo from Earle Liederman)

America's obsession with abs may be explained by the little known fact that a person with strong midsection muscles is generally pretty strong all over. Vasily Alexeyev, a Russian weightlifting icon whom *Sports Illustrated* hailed as 'the strongest man in the world' a couple of decades ago, made a big deal about training his waist muscles because he believed they were the weak link limiting everyone's performance. He told an *L. A. Times* reporter that a lifter needs abs "so strong that they can stop a bullet, but don't print that. Somebody might try."

He was right; shortly after the Great Patriotic War, as World War II is know in Russia, Soviet scientists discovered that while in low intensity movements most work is performed by the extremities, when the load is significant, the core muscles take over much of the work. "The strength of the low back and abdomen is the key to lifting big weights," agrees Yuri Spinov, two times world champion powerlifter from the Ukraine.

And as if doing their fair share during maximal squats and deads was not enough, the abs amplify the strength of other key muscles as well. Intensely contracting abdominals send nerve impulses to other muscles which starts a chain reaction. Martial artists know that flexing the abs adds more umpph to any punch or kick. Neural commands—or chi, if you prefer the Chinese terminology—transmitted by the tensed abdominals reach your quads, triceps, etc. and make them stronger!

▼

"The strength of the low back and abdomen is the key to lifting big weights," agrees Yuri Spinov, two times world champion powerlifter from the Ukraine.

▲

WARNING!

US physicians generally do not approve breath holding during exertion. Elevated internal pressure can be dangerous to your health and life! Discuss the appropriate for you exercise breathing pattern with your physician.

▼

Lives there a man with breath so dread...

—A. Smith

▲

Maximally tensed abs and obliques also elevate your intra-abdominal and intra-thoracic pressure which fortifies any exertion. There is a positive relationship between your inside pressure and your power, a so-called pneumo-muscular reflex. Somehow this pressure potentiates muscle excitability. In non-geek words, it amplifies your strength. Karate masters understood this phenomenon centuries ago. They learned to synchronize their strikes with a forceful 'Ki-ai!' Sudden forcing of the air out by a powerful contraction of the respiratory muscles and the abs peaked the internal pressure at the moment of the impact. This maneuver dramatically increases the muscular tension, or force, for a fraction of a second. That gives you a hint why heavy weight boxers are yet to break the punching power record registered on a dynamometer by a hundred thirty pound Japanese karate master.

The problem is, a bench press lasts a lot longer than a karate punch. Following the expiration the pressure drops to zero, and so does your power. I was reminded of this fact when I arm-wrestled a Harley Davidson type recently. 'Don't let me hear you breathe," warned the longhaired biker, with forearms that could be featured in a spinach commercial. To make his point the veteran arm bender pinned my arm in a flash of inside pressure, forearm tattoos a blue blur—just as I finished exhaling.

So unless you perfectly synchronize your expiration with the effort, you will get buried the same way I got pinned to the arm-wrestling table. Then what's a poor boy to do if he wants a strength boost of high internal pressure?—Hold his breath!

It is the most natural thing to do when one is exerting himself. But will it kill you, as the fitness instructor at your health club, a big brain with twelve grades of public education, has warned you?

Here is what Prof. Verkhoshansky and Dr. Siff have to say: "Many medical and other authorities state that one should never hold the breath when training with weights. This well-meaning, but misinformed, advice can lead to serious injury... the breath-holding (or Valsalva) maneuver increases the pressure in your abdomen and supports your lower spine. Without breath-holding, far greater pressure is exerted on vulnerable structures of the lumbar spine, in particular the intervertebral disks and ligaments. Prolonged breath-holding (of more than a few seconds) causes a dramatic increase in blood-pressure, followed by a sudden drop in this pressure after exhalation, so it is definitely not advisable for everyone, particularly older folk and those with cardiovascular disease."

Talk to your doctor before deciding how you breathe during exercise. I have no desire to see your family lawyer should you decide to check out in the middle of your workout. If the Doc is down on breath holding, run this alternative by him or her: "...drive up and blast out the air at the same time... Think of your mouth as the nozzle of a garden hose and... begin to exhale in a narrow, high-pressure stream. As you get past the sticking point, open your mouth wide (just like the nozzle on a hose) and empty your lungs as quickly as you can." This is the advice of Randall Strossen, a Stanford Ph.D. and a man of great knowledge of modern and vintage strength training. Make sure to save some air to stabilize your spine at the completion of an exercise, especially the deadlift!

The talk about spine stabilization brings up the issue of lifting belts. A belt restrains your inside pressure which makes you stronger via the pneumo-muscular reflex and protects your spine. Imagine surrounding your spine with a tire and then pumping the latter up. The air compressed inside your body by the belt has that effect.

It does not mean that you should ever wear a belt though. In *Back to the Future*, Part III a grizzled gun fighter broke his knuckles against Michael J. Fox's stomach cleverly protected by a cast iron plate. Today's gym rat follows Marty McFly's slick tradition and protects his soft underbelly with a foot wide armored belt. Big mistake. Containment of the internal pressures is part of the midsection muscles' job description. Consistent use of a belt, especially not backed up with proper ab training, creates a weak link in the midsection. A powerlifter acquaintance of mine who decided to try himself in a 'raw' meet which does not allow belts found out to his surprise that his abs gave out before his legs! Say no to artificial lifting aids and develop a 'virtual belt' out of rock hard abs like Yuri Spinov, the human crane from the Ukraine who does not bother to wear any belt at all, even when he squats 914!

Here is an abdominal exercise recommended by Prof. Vladimir Zatsiorsky, a leading Russian strength authority who betrayed the Dark Side of the Force and immigrated to the US. The ex-Soviet professor cites a double-blind study that showed this type of exercise to be superior any other.

After a normal inhalation—earlier Soviet research by Vorobyev recommends 75% of your maximal air intake—contract your abs while keeping your glottis closed and the rectal sphincter contracted. Expel your air forcefully in three to five seconds. Make fists if it helps you (just another demonstration of your body's interdependence and how to use it to your advantage). You can make this drill even more effective the karate way by adding a grunt after you have supposedly expelled all your air.

▼
Today's gym rat follows Marty McFly's slick tradition and protects his soft underbelly with a foot wide armored belt.
▲

The prof recommends ten to fifteen contractions per set, three to four sets spread throughout the day, every day. You know me. I would double the sets and halve the reps.

Strong abs also happen to be the best insurance policy against hernias, according to Zatsiorsky. Like a submarine hull, they should stop your guts from protruding. The professor states that comrades with strong backs but weak stomachs face the highest risk of hernias. So it may be a good idea to practice his drill for awhile before pulling really heavy deadlifts.

Zatsiorsky's Shaolin fighting monk style drill will not only strengthen your abs, but also the diaphragm and other muscles that generate high intra-abdominal pressure. It will teach you how to use them to contain the pent up pressure inside you and not let your gut hang out when you lift (a no-no!). This skill comes in handy for minimizing your odds of back injuries and hernias.

Naturally, your overall strength is increased via the pneumo-muscular reflex. Mas Oyama, a Japanese karate master famous for battling bulls unarmed and chopping their horns off barehanded (!), regularly practiced drills of this type to build up his might. If you are heavily into abs, you will find many unique midsection exercises from full contact karate, old time strong men, and the X-files labs of Eastern Europe in my book *Beyond Crunches: Hard Science. Hard Abs.* Call Dragon Door Publications at (800) 899-5111 and order a copy!

The rectal sphincter contraction recommended by Zatsiorsky as a part of his abdominal drill not only increases the inside pressure and amplifies one's strength, it also acts as an insurance against hemorrhoids. People inexperienced in lifting correctly tend to let their intestines go when they strain. Such a style of lifting could lead to hemorrhoids and offers no performance advantage. It is interesting that Chinese Chi Kung masters have been pulling their anuses up during their esoteric practices for centuries.

To sum up the eight effective breathing habits for lifting weights:

1) Clear my recommendations with your doctor.
2) Inhale 75–100% of your max lung capacity before loading your muscles.
3) Hold your breath (keep your glottis closed) as you are lowering and lifting the weight. Exhale near the end of a rep, or right after it.
4) In exercises which allow a safe relaxed pause on the bottom, for example situps or curls, you may exhale and inhale again before reversing the movement. One breathing cycle for each half rep instead of a full rep.
5) Do not expel all of your air, or you will lose tightness and stability following the exhalation.
6) Feel free to take a few breaths between your reps, but do not hyperventilate.
7) Keep your midsection rock hard but do not let your stomach bulge out.
8) Always use the anal lock (contract your rectal sphincter).

The last word on breathing and weight training safety. I cannot guarantee that you will not get hurt or killed whether you follow my advice or not. Just keep in mind that people who never lifted anything that could be classified as 'heavy' got hernias from coughing and died from a stroke when they strained on a toilet. As someone smart said, fear of doing things does not prevent you from dying, only from living.

Bodybuilders say that you should concentrate on working the muscles instead of lifting the weight. It does not have to be either or. The unique feature of the *Power to the People!* program is its techniques simultaneously maximize the training effect, safety, and performance!

"By and large, people do not get injured from using too much weight... people get injured because of their behavior—with a heavy or light weight," states Ken Hutchins who crusades for extremely slow strength exercise performance.

"Go to your car and lift it... begin to evenly apply force. Apply force, gradually increasing to a maximum force over a duration of 10 seconds or so, sustaining the maximum for several additional seconds, continuing to ventilate [indeed, holding your breath for 10 seconds is a bad idea. –P.T.], sustaining the maximum for several additional seconds, continuing to ventilate, then slowly decreasing the force and relaxing.

"Did you hurt your back? No... But what if I simply commanded you to lift your car—without the detailed instruction and admonishments to slowly apply and let off the force? The typical reaction is to yank and heave at the resistance. And this behavior—not the weight of the car—commonly results in injury."

Apart from safety, there are many reasons to lift and lower your weights slowly: three to five seconds on the way up and three to five on the way down is the *Power to the People!* rule. First, muscular tension drops off as the velocity increases. Considering that tension is what we are after, it is a dumb idea. Just note that the athletes with the most spectacular muscular definition are those from sports requiring slow exertions, such as gymnastics.

Second, contrary to what you might think, you will not be able to lift more weight if you jerk it. Ballistic cheating helps only when you lift light, Barbie and Ken weights that can be thrown in one burst of effort. You cannot do it with the mother of all weights. Watch a powerlifter deadlift 600 pounds. You will see him slowly building up tension at the start, then strain for a few seconds until the bar bends and reluctantly leaves the ground, like a space shuttle taking off. He then will grind through the rest of the lift, which might take as long as five seconds.

▼

Impatiently rushing produces no result.

—Chinese proverb

▲

Neurogeeks know of a phenomenon called a firing rate burst. If you jerk the bar, you have an immediate surge of power followed by complete muscular relaxation. If you did not succeed in throwing the barbell to lockout in one heave, you have failed. If the powerlifter in the above example tried to jerk 600 pounds, even if he did not get hurt, he would just budge the barbell a few inches off the ground where it would run out of momentum and crash down. He could not generate enough momentum to throw the weight to the top and his neurophysiology did not let him switch gears and grind the weight the rest of the way.

Studies of the bench press kinematics revealed that second rate powerlifters gunned the barbell from their chests and died half way through the lift. Top dogs, on the other hand, started slow and finished the lift with steady confidence. Yes, safety and performance are the two sides of the same coin!

Ironically, a show-off who is used to heaving and jerking his barbells fails miserably when confronted with a heavy weight. Studies show that when he attempts a ballistic lift but the weight is too heavy to cooperate, his muscles feel impotent, his nervous system panics and shuts down the operation: the barbell stays welded to the ground. On the other hand, scientists determined that a person who treats the weight the way the super slow advocate recommends lifting cars, finishes the lift. He builds up tension slowly and steadily, without what Hutchins calls 'off/oning'— and will surprise everyone with his strength once he has to demonstrate it.

Once the weight stops or nearly stops moving, the nervous system of a jerky lifter or a non-lifter interprets this event as a failed attempt and calls it quits. Slow lifting teaches the nervous system not to give up when the gravity seems to be getting the upper hand. As a powerlifting teenage national champion whom I consulted put it, 'You've gotta learn how to grind!'

▼

A show-off who is used to heaving and jerking his barbells fails miserably when confronted with a heavy weight.

▲

Feed-forward tension—how to acquire the strength of the mentally deranged

I want you to do a test. Take an empty pitcher and stick it under a faucet while holding it with a bent arm. Turn on the water and look away. Without any conscious thought on your part, your biceps will progressively tense up to hold up the heavier pitcher.

Now another experiment. Ask a friend to lift an empty suitcase but warn him that it is very heavy. He will brace himself for an effort, and grab the suitcase. Powered by excessive force, the suitcase will fly into the air. Without thinking, your friend will immediately take it easy to make his effort appropriate for the load at hand.

The intensity of a muscular contraction is the sum of 'Go!' and 'Stop!' commands coming from your brain and other parts of the nervous system such as various sensors in your muscles and tendons. Your spinal cord is constantly processing information from these proprioceptors about the resistance and joint angles. Then it makes the necessary corrections in your muscular efforts to make them appropriate for the situation at hand, such as ordering your biceps to contract harder as the pitcher is getting heavy with tap water.

It is an efficiently run feed-back operation designed to prevent you from looking like a fool when you slap an ice-cream cone into your face or try to lift a very heavy object with a dainty move, little finger sticking out. Unfortunately, this slick computerized system becomes a detriment to displaying your maximal strength. Once the resistance approaches what you believe is your maximum, the feed-back loop starts acting up. Fearing a tendon injury, it sends very powerful 'Brake!' comands to your muscles.

▼

Act like your light lifts are heavy, so your heavy lifts will feel light.

—Frantz's Third Commandment of Powerlifting

▲

1. The Feed-Back Loop   2. Feed-Forward Training

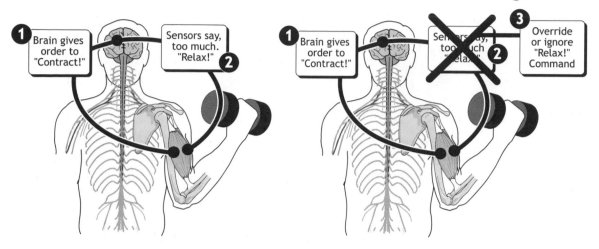

Because your strength generally does not exceed 30% of your tendon structural strength, the strength governor mechanism is set up way too conservatively. Scientists believe that pulling the brake from under your gas pedal, that is minimizing the inhibitory input into the muscles is the key that will open the door to super-strength undreamed of by the strongest people in the world. Desperate grandmothers wrestling leopards and mothers lifting cars to save their progeny supposedly do something to prevent the 'take it easy, you might get hurt!' commands from reaching their muscles. Insane people bend metal bars in the windows of their cells—I believe, they call them 'wards' in the US—because their neural circuitry is goofed up. It does not recognize the inhibitory input and does not hold you back. This is the essence of disinhibition training, the hottest new direction in strength training. Of course, we do not want to totally lose our senses, rather learn to ignore them when we choose to.

Enter feed-forward tension, one of the most promising disinhibition techniques. It requires that you maximally contract all your muscles with a submaximal weight—or no weight whatsoever! Remember Charles Atlas and his 'dynamic tension' method? You were supposed to imitate lifting a weight by flexing your muscles for all you have got. Just as Tai Chi Chi Kung differs from visually similar calisthenics in concentration and awareness, dynamic tension is an Oscar winning pantomime of a world record powerlift, and not just mindless going through the motions.

▼

Scientists believe that pulling the brake from under your gas pedal, that is minimizing the inhibitory input into the muscles is the key that will open the door to super-strength.

▲

Bodhidharma, the semi-mythical progenitor of the Oriental martial arts from India is credited with developing the Yi Ji Jing—dynamic tension exercises. They were a series of postures demanding forced tension developed a millennium and a half ago. Shown at right is one of them called Pull Bull's Tail. Bodhidharma supposedly developed them to help his weak and sickly monks to strengthen their bodies.

▼

a Soviet study by Kovalik established beyond the shadow of a doubt that 'virtual lifting' builds strength, even in so called quick lifts!

▲

The guy in a leopard skin swimsuit did not invent this method. Russian scientists Anokhin and Proshek did in the early 1900s. Or so they thought. Bodhidharma, the semi-mythical progenitor of the Oriental martial arts from India, may have practiced such exercises a millennium and a half ago. Scientists were skeptical of dynamic tension for awhile, suspecting that by creating artificial resistance within your muscles you learn to put on the brakes. Then a Soviet study by Kovalik established beyond the shadow of a doubt that 'virtual lifting' builds strength, even in so called quick lifts!

High values of muscular tension was one reason, but today we can think of another. Maximally tensing the muscles in the absence of resistance or with a light weight is only possible when the subject ignores the feed-back offered by his muscles and tendons, namely, that there is no resistance to contract against. The opposite of a normal feed-back operation, the feed-forward tension technique of maximally contracting the muscles regardless of the weight, should build superhuman strength! Once the muscles are subjected to a very heavy load, they will be able to successfully ignore the reality and lift the damn thing! Keep in mind that you must lift real heavy weights at least some of the time. Martial arts masters who practice sanchin or 'Iron Shirt' exercises know that they must break things or otherwise strike solid objects to realize the power built with dynamic tension. Your joints and connective tissues must get stronger as well as your muscles—for them virtual resistance will not cut it!

In a conversation with the super slow guy Ken Hutchins his associate Keith Johnson, M.D., coined the word 'internalization' for concentrating on the process of lifting the weight instead of the results: "They urge you to beat the equipment, as… a competitor you must defeat. They teach you to externalize a feigned aggression. You do the opposite. You seem to advocate reaching inside your body. When exercising he [Hutchins' subject] seems to turn off his surrounding environment and concentrate into an internalized trance. That's the fitting word: 'internalize'." Compare that with externalizing the effort against the barbell. Keep in mind that if you do the 'internal' gig in the context of *The Power to the People!* techniques, the 'external' results, that is the weight of the barbell lifted, will also be at its max! We accept no compromises.

The Balance of Power

STRENGTHS	WEAKNESSES

1. A command to contract the muscle from the brain
2. Hyperirradiation, the pneumomuscular and other strength promoting reflexes
3. Psychological inhibition, fear
4. Physiological inhibition, the feedback loop

Although I have quoted advocates of super slow exercise performance a few times in this book, I must make it clear that I do not subscribe to Ken Hutchins' school of strength training. In a nutshell—or 'in a nutcase' as I used to say in my early years in America—the trademarked Super Slow exercise protocol requires that one lifts the weight in ten seconds and lowers it in five. Such exaggerated slowness demands that you hold back the force output and necessitates the use of a very light weight. Muscular tension—and the results—are compromised.

The Power to the People! lifts are slow—about three to five seconds to lift, same to lower—because maximal tension of all the musculature emulates a maximal lift which usually takes that long. There is no need to time yourself. Full body tension will take care of slowing you down. Try moving fast when all your muscles are flexed—you just cannot! Compared to Super Slow, or any other exercise protocol for that matter, ***The Power to the People!* program produces superior results because it allows the highest levels of tension, full body involvement, and employs heaviest weights.** In fairness to Hutchins, he makes many excellent points, especially regarding strict exercise performance, and his protocol has some bodybuilding and rehab applications.

Feed-forward tension is not the same thing as 'feeling the muscle' either. Feeling your entire body cease to be a carbon based life form and get compressed to the density of a black hole is more like it!

When I first arm-wrestled a professional, I got annihilated. The fellow loaded his muscles with maximum tension, to the point of shaking, before we even gripped hands. On the 'Go!' he flashed my arm to the table. When he hit me, it was too late for me to load.

Speed and technique of arm-wrestling notwithstanding, after some practice you will always be able to tense your muscles the hardest before they are subjected to the load.

> ▼
> **I turn myself into a rubber band, I am ready to accept the weight and toss it back up.**
>
> *—Ernie Frantz, Powerlifting World Champion*
>
> ▲

"If the body is tight it can accept any shock", explains powerlifting great Ernie Frantz who instinctively took the right track in his training and whose book *Ernie Frantz's Ten Commandments of Powerlifting* had the rare honor of being translated into Russian. "If someone were to hit you in the stomach it might hurt, but not if you tensed your stomach muscles first..." Indeed, Chinese practitioners of Iron Shirt Chi Kung would dive off an eight foot wall, land on their chests, and live to tell about it! (Call Dragon Door Publications at (800) 899-5111 to order a free catalog which features books and tapes on Chi Kung, but try to restrain yourself from jumping off walls.)

Your best bet is to get tight before you unrack the weight and keep that tension for the duration of the rep. Ernie Frantz swears that practicing tightening up his entire body throughout the day has helped his lifting (try it on your vacation when you have no access to weights). Recall that when your tendons get loaded and your joints get compressed, they start sending negative vibes to your muscles. Maximally flexing all your muscles before you get under the iron allows for a most intense, nearly-unmitigated-by-the-sissy-reflexes contraction. Once the weight is on top of you—it is too late for them to commit their strength sabotage! You should be able to keep most of the tension gained before you felt the weight, which translates into greater strength and safety.

There are other solid scientific reasons to tense up before you get under the bar and lower it. I do not need to remind you that there is a high correlation between muscular tension and strength gains. Of all combinations of the three types of contraction (overcoming, yielding, and static, or holding), a yielding contraction which followed a static one showed the highest values of tension in a late sixties Soviet study. I believe this has to do with some peculiarities of maximal force production. If you compare a muscle to a rubber band, you can understand how it gains tension when stretched. Imagine how much more snap you can load into a rubber band if you also twist it before stretching it!

Some scientists believe that this is what happens when a muscle has to produce an extraordinary amount of force. Pre-tensing to the point of cramping before getting under a barbell can be compared to twisting a rubber band after it has fully contracted. This move enables the muscle to store great amounts of elastic energy as the descending weight stretches the rubber bands and the twists in the bands on the way down. Not surprisingly, Russian research from the days of Stalin showed that the ability to store and use the tension loaded into the muscles in the yielding phase of the movement separated elite athletes from 'also-rans'. Sly Ernie Frantz must be a CIA man with an access to classified Russian research: he always knew that the key to lifting a big weight is the amount of tension built up in the muscles before the barbell is even unracked!

Tense up maximally before getting under the weight. Attempt to maintain, and even increase, this tension as you are lowering the barbell. The more tension you have stored on the way down, the easier you are going to get up.

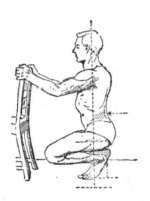

Successive induction: how to get a strong biceps by contracting your triceps

Successive induction is another one of the Sherrington Laws exploited to the max by unscrupulous Commies. According to this law, a contraction of a muscle—say, the triceps —makes its opposite number—in our case, the biceps—stronger than usual. In the early eighties scientists suggested that this maneuver has a disinhibition effect. In non-geek terms, when your triceps powerfully contract, they send the neural centers controlling the biceps a message that your bis do not have to hold back out of fear of an injury; if things get out of hand the tris are strong enough to stop them!

A year later the same group of researchers determined that a strength training program which employs the antagonist pre-tensing, or successive induction, is more effective than a conventional one. The benefits of antagonist pre-contraction do not stop at immediate performance improvement, but include lasting changes in your strength.

Like before, let the basic barbell curl be the testing range of the effects of successive induction. Perform a set of strict curls the way you were taught: butt, abs, and grip tight. Use a weight that allows about five solid reps and make sure that your elbows stay at your sides and do not drift back. Note how many reps you have done in good form.

Photo one demonstrates a regular curl with good form. The upward motion uses irradiation, good posture and breathing. But in photo two successive induction is utilized as well. Use the triceps to pull the weight down.

Rest for five minutes and do another set of curls with the same weight, but employ the new trick. Instead of lowering the barbell with the braking strength of your biceps, try to 'push' the weight down and away from you with your triceps. You are guaranteed to squeeze out an extra rep or two with this technique! These reps will be super strict because now you have two 'motors' to control the weight instead of one.

Incidentally, the successive induction maneuver offers superior joint stabilization because of the co-contraction of the muscles on both sides of it. Thus it dramatically reduces the joint stress. Encourage a friend with joint problems to discuss this powerful technique with his or her doctor. Chances are, you will be owed a big favor!

There is a Russian joke about a guy who wore shoes two sizes too small for him. When asked about his bizarre behavior, he complained about his miserable life and concluded that his only happiness in life was to come home and take off his shoes! You will be even happier than this dude if you lose yours—at least when you lift.

"Running shoes or any shock-absorbing shoes suitable for the aerobics class are potentially unsafe in the gymnasium," warn Prof. Verkhoshansky and Dr. Siff. "For instance, compression of any part of the sole during... deadlifts, standing presses... and other standing exercises can cause general instability and consequent injury. Moreover, inappropriate height of the heel can shift the center of gravity of the body forward, thereby increasing the stress on the knee joint and altering the optimal patterns of movement for safe, maximal lifts from the ground. These are all major reasons why powerlifters often wear thin heel-less shoes much like ballet pumps."

> ▼
>
> **Sometimes you have to look reality in the eye and deny it.**
>
> *—Garrison Keillor*
>
> ▲

There is more. The forcefulness of a muscular contraction is determined by the sum of the mental effort and various reflexes. When you wind up your shoulder to pitch a baseball you take advantage of the stretch reflex. Another power boosting reflex is called the positive support reaction. This reflex causes the leg musculature to contract in response to the pressure on the sole of your foot. It is a protective measure against loading.

Research suggests that always wearing shoes diminishes the sensitivity of the foot, which may turn off the strength friendly reflex. Too bad, because when the barbell is intent on squashing you like a bug on the windshield, you could use any help you can get! The only iron man who has recognized this problem is Dr. Fred Clary from Minnesota, a human crane who has elevated 900 pounds. Fred regularly performs heavy, 1,000 pounds plus, squat walkouts barefoot 'just to fire off those receptors'. Clary believes that such training sensitizes the extensor reflex receptors and enables him to lift heavier.

You do not have to walk around with half a ton on your shoulders, but you sure could lose your sneakers on steroids. Since the gym owner might object to your going native with your dirty toe nails scraping his floor, get yourself a pair of 'deadlift slippers' from Crain's Muscle World, (800) 272-0051. They look almost like ballet slippers and are probably available in pink. Have fun.

Another option is flat shoes with non-giving soles, for instance Chuck Taylor's Converse old fashioned basketball shoes. Many elite powerlifters favor this understated hard core design. You can get a pair for around thirty bucks in any athletic shoe store. Your Gramps must have worn a pair of these canvas-topped classics. They have a flat thin sole which helps your performance and safety.

Scientists believe that that running, aerobic, and other fancy shoes cause injuries which would not have happened without them! It is a fact that barefoot populations of the countries with nice climates and no extradition suffer fewer running injuries than Americans and others who look up to Amelda Marcos. The extensor reflex recruits the leg muscles in a precise pattern according to the direction of pressure from the ground. Poorly designed shoes may redirect the pressure where it does not belong and alter the proper recruitment pattern.

Besides, shoes with high shock absorption delay the transmission of pressure to the sole of your foot. That has the effect of a devious KGB trick devised to find out if a person who pretends to be deaf, is really deaf. The men in black have the American spy suspect read a script into a microphone and feed it back to his head-phones with a slight delay. This will not phase a deaf guy but will totally confuse the enemy of the state who is faking it. He will stumble and will be unable to continue. The cushy soles of your workout shoes, thick as the platforms hippie girls wore at Woodstock, will play the same joke on your extensor reflex. Although the consequences, a reduced deadlift poundage and increased odds of injury, are less drastic than a firing squat in Lubyanka courtyard, this is considered a problem in this land of minor inconveniences.

The Chuck Taylors, probably the best all around shoes for weight training, do not offer a lot of give in the soles, which improves your survival odds.

By the same token, say good-bye to your pink lifting gloves. The positive support reaction is present in your arms too when you do pressing exercises. "The human body has a number of... reflexes that serve mainly to protect the body from injury. It has been shown, for example, that pressure... near the fleshy part of the palm on the little finger side... causes extensor or stabilization response in the upper arm. This reflexively aids in stability of the whole upper arm by stimulating greater contraction of the... triceps," explains biomechanics expert and seasoned powerlifter Dr. Thomas McLaughlin.

▼

The cushy soles of your workout shoes, thick as the platforms hippie girls wore at Woodstock, will play a bad joke on your extensor reflex.

▲

Gloves reduce the pressure against your hands and sabotage your presses in the same fashion tennis shoes mess with your deadlifts. On the other hand, holding the bar with bare hands in the manner suggested by Dr. McLaughlin — "You will be surprised if you try this at how powerful and comfortable this maneuver makes the arm feel." —and squeezing it hard will up your power!

Having disposed of gloves and cushy sneakers, let us send gym mirrors the way of the Berlin Wall!

▼

Robert Roman's sportsmen develop their muscle-joint sense by lifting ...blindfolded!

▲

Prof. Robert Roman used to conquer gold for the Soviet Empire on the weightlifting platform. Today he is a top coach who has trained many young lifters to greatness using his revolutionary methods. Roman is convinced that developing superior sport specific body awareness will make a difference between being good and great!

It is not enough to have muscle, you have got to know how to use it. Soviet experiments revealed that even elite lifters made huge errors in estimating the height of the lift, the magnitude of the force, etc. When special techniques for maximizing what Roman calls the 'muscle-joint sense' were developed, the top guys outdid themselves and some unpromising also-rans became world class!

Robert Roman's sportsmen develop their muscle-joint sense by lifting ... blindfolded! Their coach explains that because we so heavily rely on our eyesight, we do not pay enough attention to the various sensations in our muscles, tendons, ligaments, and joints. When blindfolded, the lifter is forced to listen to his body. Contrary to what a mirror gazing bodybuilder wants to believe, this tremendously improves the technique and its stability!

Kick off your muscle-joint sense training by getting a pair of air-line blindfolds. Roman does not recommend lifting with your eyes closed because it distracts you from what you are supposed to be doing. Training with the lights turned off may be an effective alternative, but the gym owner might object, at least if he finds you before he stumbles on a dumbell and cracks his head against the Smith machine. So blindfolds it is.

Start deadlifting or pressing light with your eyes open, then cover your eyes. Keep alternating open and shut eye sets or reps but do not add wheels until you own a given weight blind. Do not just go through the motions but concentrate on various feed-back your body has to offer: muscular tension, joint angles, etc. When something feels wrong, correct it and remember what you have corrected.

The purpose of this drill is not to make your deadlifts pretty, but to make them heavy. By finessing your skill, you are guaranteed to lift a lot more iron. Just ask four times Powerlifting World Record Holder Dr. Judd Biasiotto who spent a lot of time developing his squatting body awareness with special techniques of his own. "...I was able to become aware of the muscles I was using during each segment of my lifts. When I got stuck at a certain part of the lift, I knew exactly which muscles to recruit and/or concentrate on to make the lift." And stood up with 605 pounds at 130 pounds of bodyweight! Have no doubt that his proprioceptive sensitivity training paid off.

Even if you do not muster the courage to lift blindfolded once in awhile, at least stop using mirrors. A friend of mine was squatting in a health spa which had more mirrors than a Las Vegas hotel room and hurt his back, confused and distracted by the reflections.

Mirrors, gloves, belts, and fancy sneakers are expensive and dangerous distractions from effective training. Just say no. If you can't, get help.

▼
Mirrors, gloves, belts, and fancy sneakers are expensive and dangerous distractions from effective training. Just say no. If you can't, get help.
▲

"When I'm done with you," I promised to the new batch of hard asses in the Soviet Special Forces, or *Spetsnaz,* "You will have the flexibility of a mutant. Or else."

The storm troopers of the Evil Empire knew that a muscle that can easily relax into an extreme stretch is a muscle that can do things. Hit hard and fast, lift heavy, never quit, never hurt, blast into action without warm-up, and recover from it overnight. Deprived of food and sleep, exhausted from every exertion known to man, bloodied in full contact hand-to-hand combat, we still did things like one arm chins and ten foot standing broad jumps all in a day's work.

Do you want to get super strong and live to tell about it? Start stretching the Russian way, Comrade! You will say good-bye to most aches and pains which veteran weight trainers put up with as a part of the game. You will recover from your bar bending deadlifts twice as quick as your friends and you will get stronger faster.

And do not forget the cliché that stretching improves your odds against injuries. You cannot add another inch to your chest if your shoulders scream in pain and you are forced to reduce your benching poundage by fifty pounds. And you cannot do much of anything, least of all get strong, if your back punishes you with an electric shock every time you move.

"I stretched my spine in every workout and with every available exercise," recalls Soviet weightlifting legend Yuri Vlasov who could bend over with his knees locked and touch his head to his shins. "Because I stuck to this rule religiously, in all my years in the big sport I never knew the back pains so common to athletes."

Ironically, all of the above does not mean that you should stretch or warm up BEFORE your lifting. At the most do a couple of lighter sets of two to three reps just to get in the groove. Even that, in my not so humble opinion, is an overkill. You have started your power cycle with light weights and by the time you are moving heavy iron you should have developed acceptable technique. Understand that you might get injured whether you warm up and stretch or not. As the French say, *C'est la vie!,* such is life.

If you want to know why I am down on warming up and pre-workout stretching, please read my *Beyond Stretching: Russian Flexibility Breakthroughs* book. It is also the source for state of the art flexibility techniques decades ahead of the lame 'relaxed stretches' and 'active isolated stretches' popular in this country.

In addition to the mentioned health management benefits, scientific stretching can make you a lot stronger and, if that is your desire, slap on some serious meat on your bones! Did you know that the most dramatic muscle growth on this planet

▼

I'm only a hamstring tear away from oblivion.

—Steve Jones

▲

took place in a chronically stretched muscle? In slightly over a month of progressively more intense stretching the mass of a bird's wing muscle increased by an out of this world 334%! Stretching induced muscle damage appears to trigger muscle cell splitting, or hyperplasia. Although all the bugs have not been worked out for humans yet, the possibilities are awesome!

In a 1977 study by Yefimov, Russian weightlifters reported an average 9.4% strength increase when they added special Loaded Passive Stretches between their sets. In a recent US study by Westcott the subjects who stretched the muscles they have just worked with a strength exercise for twenty seconds gained almost 20% more strength than the group that did not stretch in the end of a ten week program! Dr. Wayne Westcott could not explain why but suggested that contraction and stretching are the two functions of a muscle, and by not training one of them you sell yourself short on the other one as well. The Yin and Yang of muscle function.

Then why, you might ask, are most stretching fanatics such pencilnecks? Because they are stretching wrong. Russian hand-to-hand combat instructor Vlad Fadeyev made a point that a fighting man cannot afford the rag doll looseness developed with Western stretching systems. Neither can you. The alternative: stretch the Russian way!

In Eastern European sports science stretching is considered to be a form of strength training. It is, if you do it right. Take Plyometric Flexibility Training. It increases your muscles' and tendons' ability to store energy like a coiled spring. It is elementary, Watson. If you can load more tension into your pecs and delts when you are lowering a heavy bench, you will be able to lift more as well. In an Australian study a group of experienced powerlifters who stretched their shoulder girdles twice a week gained an average of fifteen pounds on their bench in only eight weeks!

Some state of the art flexibility drills, especially Shutdown Threshold Isometrics and Fascial Stretching, make you stronger by as much as 20% through desensitizing the Golgi tendon organs. The GTOs are the governors limiting your strength. These tiny sensors in your connective tissues shut down the muscles once they register a force that exceeds their limit. Do the right stretches and pull that brick from under your gas pedal!

You get the idea. Special flexibility training will help you get superstrong. **Call (800) 899-5111 and buy my book.** Or else.

On the first pages of *Power to the People!* you discovered the only power tool which can transform your body—high muscular tension. Since then you have been steadily adding power features to your tool—unique techniques like hyperirradiation, pre-tension, or successive induction which amplify tension and your gains. You have sharpened your tool with the discoveries of low rep training not to failure, cycling, and other subtle yet vital keys to success. It is time to pick up your power attachments kit—a select group of exercises which will forge your body into an off-planet rock if used in the context of the *Power to the People!* plan.

The Deadlift

Time to start by buying a 300 pound Olympic weight set: a barbell with plates. Even if you are as weak as your grandmother, still buy the whole thing (my grandmother beat me in arm-wrestling till I was fifteen). Eventually you will hopefully beat your grandmother, and, besides, the whole thing will set you back by no more than $150. Unlike Soloflex and other fancy coat hangers, hard core basics come cheap.

▼

The whole thing will set you back by no more than $150. Unlike Soloflex and other fancy coat hangers, hard core basics come cheap.

▲

Also get a rubber mat about seven feet long and three to four feet wide to protect your basement floor. About three quarters of an inch thickness should do. If you live in an apartment or an older building consider extra padding. If you are handling monstrous weights and/or you have to take extra precautions, follow the advice I got from Marty Gallagher. This powerlifting champ suggests that you get a thick sheet of plywood and set it on top of four old tires of the same size. No, the contraption does not feel like a water bed, promises Gallagher. Hammer a couple two by fours on the edges of the plywood parallel to the barbell. These lips should stop the bar from rolling off. Cover the works with a rubber mat. An overkill for most, salvation for some.

Set your shiny new bar on the mat and load it up with small plates. When you are loading the bar, make sure to keep your back straight and avoid twisting:

Develop good habits while the weights are light. Do not get sloppy. It is not the poundage, but poor alignment that gets you injured. Respect the weight, even if it is light.

Stand facing the bar with your feet the way you would have them for jumping: about one foot apart, with your toes pointing straight forward or slightly out. The barbell should be above the center of your feet.

Look right over your head and inhale as deeply as possible. Holding your breath, a very tight arch in your lower back, and keeping your shoulders back, slowly descend to grip the bar. If you cannot maintain the arch even without a weight, you need to work on your hamstring flexibility. Get my book *Beyond Stretching: Russian Flexibility Breakthroughs* and fix it before attempting any deads.

Stay on your heels all the time and never let your eyes leave the ceiling. Your body will follow your head. If you look down, which is what everybody tends to do, you will do all the lifting with your back, rather than your legs. A bad move.

▼

Make a point of pushing your butt back as much as possible, as if sitting in a chair which is far behind you. You will feel like you are fighting your hamstrings to get down.

▲

Make a point of pushing your butt back as much as possible, as if sitting in a chair which is far behind you. You will feel like you are fighting your hamstrings to get down. It is good, they will tighten to contract more. Try this drill: Reach out for a stool with your butt as you are descending to grab the bar.

When you are squatting going down to grip the bar, your body should feel very tight. Visualize loading a very tight spring. Skinny Lamar Gant who has deadlifted five times his bodyweight, pound for pound more than anyone in the world, swears by this technique.

Make a point of pushing your butt back as much as possible, as if sitting in a chair which is far behind you. You will feel like you are fighting your hamstrings to get down. It is good, they will tighten to contract more powerfully when you start lifting the barbell. Do not let your knees go forward, the closer your shins are to vertical, the better.

Grip the bar without looking at it; your eyes should remain fixed on the ceiling throughout the lift. If you feel that you have not gripped it evenly, it is OK to adjust your grip. as long as you do not look down. If you fail, let go of the bell, stand up, and start all over.

1. Good Form—Note: the straight back.

1. Poor Form—Note: the curved back and forward lean.

▼

Use bad form
and find out
why there is a
'dead' in
the deadlift.

▲

It is alright if you are off by an inch or so; most real life activities are not symmetrical. Just make sure to stay tight during the lift and avoid any twisting.

Grip the bar with an alternate grip. It means one palm is facing forward, and the other one back. This weird move will help you to hold on to the bar better when the weights get heavy. If you have ever taken a self-defense class, you know that one thumb is weaker than four fingers. That is why you were taught to push against the assailant's thumbs to break his grip around your wrists. If you use a normal overhand grip on the bar, a heavy weight will eventually make your weaker thumbs give out. A staggered grip backs your thumbs up with the

Try the alternate grip

stronger fingers of your other hand. This maneuver will initially feel unnatural but you will get used to it. Remember to switch hands on every set to even out the load.

Show time! You have held your breath, your head tilted back, and an arch in your spine all this time. Your knees are half bent and your hips are neither too high nor too low. Slowly and deliberately push the floor away with your feet, as if you are jumping in slow mo. Do not pull on the bar—you will only end up lifting it with your back and arms. Forget your arms, they are nothing but cables connecting the weight to your body. A Russian study by Sokolov determined that you lose 9% of your pulling strength if your head is down, 13% if your back is rounded, and a whopping 40% if you are pulling with bent arms! Besides, you do not strengthen your hips or thighs and risk a back injury if you are all humped over and yanking on the bar with your arms!

Flex the triceps before
grabbing the bar

Some powerlifters flex their triceps as they are reaching for the bar to assure that their arms are straight.
A good tip. Use it.

1. Poor Form—Note the angle of the shins

Poor lifting form demonstrated above. How are you going to get the bar past your knees if you pull straight up?

▼
Never twist or turn your neck when deadlifting! You are almost guaranteed a trip to a chiropractor if you do.
▲

The weight should be deliberately 'squeezed' off the floor for safe and effective deadlift performance. Your knees should point in the same direction your feet are pointing at all times. Do not let them buckle in, which could be hard on your knee ligaments. Consciously keep your knees pointed forward throughout the lift. You may even have to think of pushing them out to keep them straight!

You have heard it before: keep you abs and glutes tight! Make a point that you keep your back locked at all times and keep your weight on your heels. If you are still looking at the ceiling, or far in front of you, like you should, it should not be a problem. But never twist or turn your neck when deadlifting! You are almost guaranteed a trip to a chiropractor if you do.

The bar should stay close to your legs at all times. It helps to think of pulling the

▼
**The bar should
stay close to
your legs at
all times.
It helps to think
of pulling the
bar towards you
rather than
straight up**
▲

bar towards you rather than straight up:

If you have been doing everything by the book, by the time the bar has reached your knees, your shins should be vertical:

by the time the bar has reached your knees, your shins should be vertical

Once the bar has reached your knees, drive your hips forward while squeezing your butt

Two phases of proper form in the deadlift lock out

▼

A properly performed deadlift finish is crisp and mechanical, not flowing or draggy.

▲

hard, as if pinching a coin. At the same time throw your shoulders back while keeping your chest high and back arched. A properly performed deadlift finish is crisp and mechanical, not flowing or draggy.

You will end up standing straight with the bar hanging in your straight arms and resting against your thighs. Do not exaggerate the finish by leaning back! It only puts unhealthy stress on your spine. Flexing your abs at this point will help to prevent you from leaning back.

Time to take a breather. Exhale half your air, inhale to the hilt, and head back to earth. For most exercises the rule of thumb is to lower the weight with control. The deadlift is an exception. An attempt to slowly lower the bar tends to throw the weight forward and overstress your back.

The proper way to get the bar home is to quickly push your glutes back—sitting in a chair, remember?—and let the bar nearly fall to the floor. Sticking your butt out will move your knees out of the barbell's way. Stay on your heels all the time and do not look down!

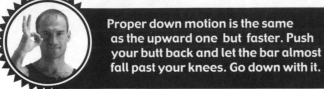
Proper down motion is the same as the upward one but faster. Push your butt back and let the bar almost fall past your knees. Go down with it.

There is scientific data suggesting that controlled lowering of the weights is more important than lifting them for making the muscle grow. Deadlift is one of the few exercises which enables you to safely drop the weight after you have lifted it. One more reason to deadlift if you want to get stronger and harder without getting husky!

Do not purposefully drop the bar, however! Your hand or hands might get stuck and might get injured. Dropping with the bar is safer. Ditto for a time when for some reason you could not make the lift. Ideally it is 'never'.

DO NOT SET THE DEADLIFT DOWN SLOWLY!
You will be pulled forward and might get hurt.

For the next rep let go of the bar, stand up and start all over. If you hang on to the bar for the duration of the set, your form will surely deteriorate, and the weight will shift from your hips and thighs onto your back.

POWER TO THE PEOPLE!

The Deadlift Highlights:

- Stay on your heels
- Keep your back arched
- Never look down
- Push the floor away
- Stay 'tight' and hold your air when lifting

The Sumo Deadlift (glute emphasis)

Don't get nervous now. You will not be breaking any bathroom scales! This deadlift is called 'sumo' because it is done with a wide stance and your arms inside your knees. Big Japanese dudes dig this stance because their thighs chafe less this way. One of the ladies I have coached insisted on calling these 'plie deadlifts' because 'sumo didn't sound feminine'. I said, what the hell, you could call it 'Bob' for all I care, just do them!

▼
Some comrades choose sumos for the pointed effect they have on their glutes.
▲

The Sumo with good form

Some comrades choose sumos for the pointed effect they have on their glutes. Others, generally long backed and short armed folk, prefer it because it is more natural for their body structure. Some world class powerlifters start a cycle with the deadlift variation which is hardest for them, be it sumo or conventional, and then switch to their strong stance as the weight gets heavier and they approach the peak. It is a solid approach to training. Consider it.

Stand with your feet comfortably wide and your toes turned out thirty to forty five degrees. You should be able to reach the bar with your knees tracking your feet. If your turnout is inadequate and you cannot, off you go stretching your groin muscles!

The Sumo with poor form

Everything that applies to the conventional deadlift works for the sumo as well. One thing different is the lockout. You may have difficulty driving your hips through with a wide stance, the bar tends to drag.

Pushing your chest out while 'pinching a coin' between your buttocks will help. Also, think that you are trying to 'get tall':

The Romanian Deadlift—A tighter back arch and less straightened than usual

The Modified Romanian Deadlift for hamstring and calf emphasis

Modify the basic deadlift with the following.

Point your feet straight forward; no turnout. Make a point of keeping your weight on your heels and keeping your shins totally vertical. Imagine that you are stuck in cement up to your knees (for a few roubles it can be arranged).

Start the pull with your knees straighter than in the conventional deadlift, and your hips higher. Your hamstrings will be toast!

The Romanian Deadlift with a book added underfoot to blast the calves and hammies

To blast your hammies even more and give your calves something to think about, stick books or boards underneath the balls of your feet.

Make sure that you have adequate flexibility before taking up these deadlift variations.

The Duck Deadlift off a platform for quad emphasis

The Duck Deadlift without a platform

The Duck Deadlift off a Platform for quad emphasis

Turn your feet and knees out approximately forty-five degrees. Make sure that they keep pointing in the same direction for the duration of the drill.

As an options stand on a solid elevation of up to four inches to lengthen the pull and make your thighs more miserable. Using small plates on your bar also does the trick.

Keep your body more upright and your hips lower than in the conventional deadlift. Get going!

The Snatch Pull for upper lats and upper back emphasis

The Snatch Pull for lats and upper back emphasis

It is a conventional deadlift with a very wide overhand grip. Make sure that your shoulders and wrists can take it.

Use what weightlifters call the 'hook grip'. Wrap your index and, if possible your middle fingers around your thumbs. The hook grip is painful, but it enables you to hold on heavy weights without resorting to the staggered powerlifting grip. Eventually most people are not bothered by it.

Do everything by the basic deadlift book, but pay special attention to keeping your shoulder blades locked together. Finish the lift with a shrug, but do not pull with your biceps.

the hook grip

The Clean Pull (grip emphasis)

It is the same thing as the conventional deadlift, except the grip. The overhand—no hook—grip makes this drill an excellent hand and forearm developer.

My favorite method of incorporating the clean pull into my training is to start a power cycle with it and switch to the staggered grip when I can no longer hold on to the weight.

The Deadlift Lockout, or the Health Lift
(midsection, traps, and grip emphasis)

The deadlift from the knee level is the same thing as 'the health-lift' of the Civil War days! If you have access to a power rack, lockouts can be very beneficial. They enable you to handle a lot of weight and work a lot of muscle.

Perform a lockout like a standard staggered grip deadlift. Make a point of starting the pull by squeezing your butt, rather than pulling with your back. Keep everything tight.

The Side Press

There are dozens of pressing movements: the bench press, the parallel bar dip, the incline dumbell press... The old-fashioned side press is the press of choice for the exclusive *Power to the People!* program for seven reasons:

1. The side press requires full body action and gives a great workout to the stabilizing muscles of the midsection, it is a long time favorite of Russian weightlifters;

2. The side press requires that you to lift a seven-foot bar with one arm, therefore it gives a great workout to the gripping and various stabilizing muscles;

3. The side press is a lot easier to learn than, say, a proper two arm military press;

4. The side press teaches good habits for overhead lifting, which come in handy in everyday life;

5. The side press places the shoulder in the position of external rotation, which enhances workout safety and strengthens the rotator cuff muscles;

6. The side press encourages the use of the lats, 'the armpit muscles', to stabilize the shoulder joint, a measure that greatly increases training safety and longevity;

7. The side press requires no spotters or any additional equipment like benches or racks.

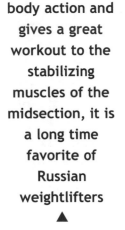

▼

The side press requires full body action and gives a great workout to the stabilizing muscles of the midsection, it is a long time favorite of Russian weightlifters

▲

The hoisting sequence prior to the side press is exercise in itself. Follow all of these steps carefully to avoid injury.

Start by tilting a barbell on its side with two hands. Make sure that the barbell collars you use are up for the task. Regular spring collars are iffy when the weight mounts; at some point consider buying a pair of top of the line weightlifting collars.

When the bar is vertical, grip its dead center with one hand, inhale, and dip down as you hoist the bar to your shoulder. Keep your body tight and never lean back.

Needless to say, for most comrades, even men, starting out with a forty-five pound seven foot bar is a tall order. A short fifteen pound 'EZ curl bar' will come in very handy. If even that is a challenge, you can start your strength training career with a small barbell plate.

Your midsection should be solid; your hip and leg muscles should be braced against the ground. Never lean back or twist!

Here is a useful drill that will teach you how to do the above. Stand inside a doorway with your feet at your shoulder width. Place one hand against the top of the doorway. Without raising your shoulder more than necessary, slowly start pushing away from the doorway with your arm and away from the floor with your legs. Keep your abs and glutes tight and breathe shallow.

In a few seconds build the tension up to its maximum. Note how powerful and stable you feel when you keep your whole body rigid instead of just pushing with your arm. Let go.

The barbell should be in the position of a press behind the neck (photo). Press your working shoulder and elbow down, as if you are hitting someone in the head. Inhale, flex your whole body as you did during the last drill, and squeeze the barbell with all you have got.

Ready to press!

Now, instead of pushing the barbell, push yourself away from the bar. This secret visualization prevents your shoulder from raising prematurely, losing power, and getting hurt.

Push away slightly sideways, so your body will lean away slightly. This move will give a great workout to your side muscles: lats, obliques, etc., and will enable you handle more weight. Leaning sideways also discourages leaning back, which is a no-no!

2. In mid-press position

Avoid any twisting when you lean! Try to keep your lats, or 'armpit muscles' tight.

2. In top position

When you have locked out your arm, let out some air and relax a little. Do not overdo it; you might expose your back or shoulder to an injury.

Inhale again, crush the barbell, and actively pull the bar down with your elbow, as if you are trying to break a brick with it.

Successive induction boosts your strength and does a lot to protect your shoulder.

Bad form in the mid-position

Your body will resume its vertical position as you lower the weight. Release some tension and air once you have brought your elbow down as low as it will go, and go for another rep.

If you choose to go with another free weight press, for example, the bench, it's alright, as long as you know how to do it right.

▼

If you choose to go with another free weight press, for example, the bench, it's alright, as long as you know how to do it right.

▲

Bad form in the start position

Having trouble with the bar, or even the EZ curl bar? Try starting out with just a small plate and work up to a 25 pound plate. Then try the bar again.

The Floor Press (pec emphasis)

The old fashioned floor press is the poor man's answer to the bench press—everybody has got some floor!

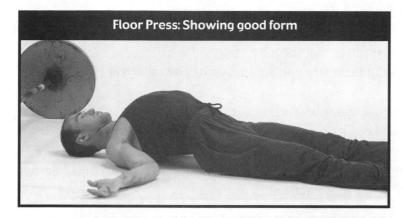

Floor Press: Showing good form

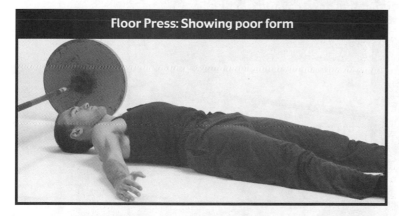

Floor Press: Showing poor form

Floor Press: The hand-off from the partner (end the same way)

Very important: your shoulders should stay pressed down into the floor and towards your feet throughout the set! Letting your shoulders roll forward or shrug up invites injury and makes for a nonproductive workout.

To get your shoulders down, force your rib cage up as high as possible while pinching an imaginary tennis ball with your shoulder blades before the spotter hands you down the weight. Your lower back will arch slightly. It is OK.

Lie on the floor with your legs straight and your feet shoulder wide. Have a training partner standing behind your head deadlift a barbell and hand it over to you. The spotter should be holding the bar while you are adjusting your grip, then help you move it over your sternum

Use a comfortable width grip. Do not go too narrow or too wide, it puts too much stress on your wrist. Shoulder width, give or take a couple of inches, is about right. Also, keep your wrists neutral; letting them hyperextend is asking for problems. If you have trouble keeping them straight, squeezing the bar tight will help.

Once you have the bar over your breast bone—not over your face or throat!—inhale maximally. While keeping your body locked, lower the barbell straight down until your elbows rest on the floor. Your forearms should be vertical at this point. It helps to think of pulling your elbows into the floor for a tight and controlled descent (photo). Powerlifters use this technique with great success.

Floor Press: Beginning descent after hand-off

Floor Press: Bad positioning—too far back. The ghosted image shows where the bar should reside—Over the breastbone.

Attempting to 'break' the bar on the way down and up will heavily involve your lats and further increase your power and safety.

Let the air out and deeply inhale one more time. Keeping your whole body rigid, squeeze the bar and push yourself away from it. Squeezing the barbell will amplify the contraction of all the involved muscles. Visualizing pushing yourself away from the bar and into the floor will help to keep your shoulders down.

Floor Press: Showing the concept of "Breaking the Bar"
Try to rotate the shoulders in commanding the lats.

Floor Press: down position.

▼
Squeezing the barbell will amplify the contraction of all the involved muscles. Visualizing pushing yourself away from the bar and into the floor will help to keep your shoulders down.
▲

The bar should move straight up. Don't curve towards your face (photo). When you lock out the weight don't try to lift it as high as possible by rolling your shoulders off the floor. (photo). Elbows have locked—and that is it, time for another rep (photo). Exhale, inhale again... well, now you know what to do.

Floor Press: Showing good beginning and ending position. From here the partner takes the weight.

The Curl Grip Floor Press
(biceps and lateral triceps emphasis)

This press is the numero uno exercise for toning up the lateral head of your triceps, or the outside of your arm. It is also very easy on the shoulder joint because the arms are tightly 'screwed' into their sockets. If you have a shoulder injury, ask the doc if this is the exercise for you.

To find the proper width for the reverse grip play with it in the starting position for the curl You will notice that your arms naturally go out to the sides instead of coming straight down.

Prepare for the floor press and assume the grip you have found most comfortable. Turn your fingers out slightly and let the bar lie in the grooves of your hands

The reverse grip press requires more control than the regular press and has a different sticking point. Be ready.

Demonstrating the curl grip for the floor press

Demonstrating the curl grip as applied to the bar

▼

This press is the numero uno exercise for toning up the lateral head of your triceps, or the outside of your arm. It is also very easy on the shoulder joint because the arms are tightly 'screwed' into their sockets.

▲

The Barbell Curl

Too tired. To argue. With American males' fatal attraction to curls. I know young Commies will do them anyway, so I might as well teach them the right way.

Lift the bar off the floor with the wider than shoulders grip you used in the last exercise. Inhale, and lock your glutes and abs. 'Brace' your feet against the ground and press your shoulders down. Keep them there for the duration of the set.

Squeeze the bar and grind out your rep. Exhale and semi-relax on the top.

Curl—begin

Curl—starting lift

▼
**Plug the curls into your workout following the deads and the presses and follow the standard cycling format.
Drop me a note when you are forced to drink your beer through a straw.**
▲

Curl—end

Inhale and tighten up again. Lower the barbell by pushing it down and away with your triceps. It is alright to let your elbows move forward slightly, but not back.

Plug the curls into your workout following the deads and the presses and follow the standard cycling format. Drop me a note when you are forced to drink your beer through a straw.

Curl—the whole nine yards

Power To The People

Manifesto

The Power to the People! Manifesto

It is rough driving down the information superhighway when everybody is pushing you a different map. Different, expensive, and awfully complicated. The fitness business has gotten to the point where one needs a background in biochemistry just to read supplement ads. Listen to the locker room talk, and you will get the impression that you are on the campus of a graduate exercise physiology school. A gym rat at the turn of the century is a walking encyclopaedia of useless knowledge. Which brand of whey protein is the best, what bench incline angle is optimal for hitting the upper pecs, what are the advantages of effervescent creatine, when is the best time of the day to do cardio, how to superset biceps curls and triceps extensions for best pump.

None of the above will forge a strong body. "I knew so much about that which I did not need, but knew so little about that which I needed," laments Stuart McRobert, a once frustrated British bodybuilder who finally discovered the Holy Grail of power, periodization plus abbreviated routines of basic exercises. "And therein lies the plight of most bodybuilding junkies."

Do you fail to see the forest from the trees? "Why do herbivores on the plains of the Savannah have eyes on the sides of their heads, whereas carnivores have them at the front?" ask biologist Jack Cohen and English professor of mathematics Ian Stewart in their awesome book The Collapse of Chaos:

Discovering Simplicity in a Complex World. *"A genuinely reductionist explanation would look deep inside the animals' cells, sequence their DNA, and describe the chemical changes that lead to eyes at the side of their heads... However, there is a very compelling "why" answer... Animals live in ecological systems, and forces from the outside cause them to evolve. Carnivores need eyes at the front in order to focus their attention on their prey as it tries to elude their clutches. Herbivores need to keep an all-around watch for predators, and that is most easily achieved with eyes on the sides."*

When the content is staggeringly complicated, look into the context.

Digging deeper into the muscle cell in an attempt to solve the strength puzzle is a clear case of dwelling on content of unessential details and forgetting the all-powerful context. The context is obvious. Your environment, real or self-imposed in the gym, demands that you get stronger. Go and lift heavier and heavier weights! It is that simple.

▼
When the content is staggeringly complicated, look into the context.
▲

Scientists who study non-linear dynamics know that complexity on one level implies simplicity on another. They even have a term, simplexity, which refers to the emergence of simple rules from underlying disorder and complexity. In Power to the People! I have attempted to deliver a 'simplex' approach to strength training, decades of scientific research and hundreds of years of lifting and martial arts experience distilled into a no frills power formula anyone, from a recent couch potato to a world class athlete, can use.

I shall finish Power to the People! *with the words Bruce Lee, a martial artist extraordinaire who cut through the unnecessary fluff of the traditional fighting arts and refined combat to brutally effective essentials:*

"Before I studied the art, a punch to me is just like a punch, a kick just like a kick. After I've studied the art, a punch is no longer a punch, a kick no longer a kick. Now that I understand the art, a punch is just a punch, a kick is just a kick."

Get to work!

About the Author
Pavel Tsatsouline
Master of Sports

Pavel Tsatsouline, Master of Sports, is a former physical training instructor for Spetsnaz, the Soviet Special Forces, an articulate speaker, and an iconoclastic authority on flexibility and strength training.   Pavel was nationally ranked in the Russian ethnic strength sport of kettle-bell lifting and holds a Soviet Physical Culture Institute degree in physiology and coaching. Tsatsouline has authored three books, *Beyond Stretching, Beyond Crunches,* and *Power to the People!*

'The Evil Russian' also spreads Communist sports and fitness training propaganda through tailored workshops in a variety of athletic, corporate, and public settings. For seminar availability please e-mail to Pavelizer@aol.com or write to:

ADVANCED FITNESS SOLUTIONS, Inc.
P.O. Box 65472
St. Paul, MN 55165
or
pavelizer@aol.com

Be the Proud Owner of a Dynamically Responsive Body— at Any Age!

- Learn to wake up your proprioceptors in a hurry— for a vibrant start to the day and to stop feeling like the Tin Man when you get up in the morning.
- Learn techniques to increase blood flow to your joints, lubricate them and keep their surfaces smooth and healthy, for pain-free, easy movement on a daily basis.
- Learn the difference between plyometric and dynamic stretching—when to use the one, when to use the other for optimal gains.
- Learn special techniques developed by Dr. Fred Hatfield, the first man to officially squat over 1,000 pounds.
- Learn the right way and right time to perform shake outs for optimal results in martial arts, plus some special cautionsthat will save you injury and bad kicking habits.
- Learn <u>twenty nine joint mobility and dynamic stretch exercises</u> with full descriptions and photographs.
- Learn <u>twenty two isometric stretches</u> with full descriptions and photographs.
- Learn five additional key techniques for optimal performance with full descriptions and photographs.
- Learn why resetting the sensitivity of your stretch reflex may be the key to injury prevention.
- Learn why <u>exercise machines can spell disaster for your body</u> and why ballistic movement is the natural and safest way to workout.
- Learn why dynamic stretching is so much more effective than slow stretching.
- Learn how Dr. Judd Biasiotto surpassed ten state power lifting records without using a warm up.
- Learn why isometric stretching is 267% more effective than conventional relaxed stretching.
- Learn this surefire technique guaranteed to make your tendons thicker and stronger—a must for any martial artist or serious athlete.
- Learn how plyometric stretching increases your strength with a <u>zero increase in muscle mass.</u>
- Learn how Digital Fascial Planing can increase your strength by up to 20%.
- Learn why you should never try to stretch your ligaments, and the danger signals to listen for.
- Learn how the Russian principle of accentuation develops strength in the range where you really need it for your chosen sport.

> "*You are not training if you are not training with Pavel!*"
>
> —Dr. Fred Clary, National Powerlifting Champion and World Record Holder.

Order the companion video:

Beyond Stretching

By Pavel Tsatsouline #V51
30 min.—$29.95

Fast-paced, nitty-gritty demonstrations of many of the most essential techniques shown in Pavel's breakthrough book.

"Abs to Die For—Secrets to Kill For."

Gain a Ripped Powerhouse of Six-Pack Muscle
In No Time at All—with Breakthrough Techniques
That Blow the Roof Off Traditional Ab Exercises

BEYOND CRUNCHES:
HARD SCIENCE. HARD ABS.

By Pavel Tsatsouline
8½" x 11" 128 pages, over 82 photographs—$34.95 #B08

Employ These Little-Known Tips from Elite Athletes and Possess Your Own Set of Awesome Abs

- Protect your back and develop exceptional abdominal muscle tone, with a landmark exercise designed for the special needs of Russian ballet dancers and gymnasts.

- Employ the secret ab weapon of an old time strongman—famous for his exceptional strength and sinewy, wiry physique.

- This insider's secret from East German research radically empowers the traditional situp.

- Russian full contact fighters used this drill to pound their opponents with organ-rupturing power, while turning their own midsections into concrete. Unlike anything seen in the US!

- This simple Yoga asana tightens the internal muscles of the abdominal wall and makes your waist smaller—even if you have not lost a pound!

"As a chiropractic physician, I see the deleterious effects of a weak torso on the lower back. Weak abs lead to years of back pain and dysfunction. As a world record holding powerlifter, I know the importance of strong abs on maximum power performance. *Beyond Crunches* is THE text and authority on ab/trunk stability." —*Dr. Fred Clary*

1-800-899-5111
24 HOURS A DAY
FAX YOUR ORDER (970) 872-3862

Yes, I Want My Fried Abs NOW!— I'm Done Wasting My Time with Slow Burns and Half-Baked Results

As a former Soviet Union Special Forces conditioning coach, Pavel Tsatsouline already knew a thing or two about how to create bullet-stopping abs. Since then, he has combed the world to pry out this select group of primevally powerful ab exercises— guaranteed to yield the fastest, most effective results known to man. According to Pavel, "Crunches belong on the junk pile of history, next to Communism. 'Feeling the burn' with high reps is a waste of time!" Save yourself countless hours of unrewarding, if not useless—if not damaging—toil. Get with the program. Make fast gains and achieve blistering, rock-hard abs now.

Fry your abs without the spine-wrecking, neck-jerking stress of traditional crunches—using this radical situp designed by the world's leading back and muscle function expert, Professor Janda, from Czechoslovakia.

When it came to wanting titanium abs yesterday, the Soviet Special Forces didn't believe in delayed gratification. Pavel gave them what they wanted. If you want abs that'll put you in the world's top 1 percent, this cruel and unusual drill does the trick.

Russian full contact fighters used this drill to pound their opponents with organ-rupturing power, while turning their own midsections into concrete.

1-800-899-5111
24 HOURS A DAY
FAX YOUR ORDER (970) 872-3862

No one—but no one—has ever matched Bruce Lee's ripped-beyond-belief abs. What was his favorite exercise? Here it is. Now you can rip your own abs to eye-popping shreds and reclassify yourself as superhuman.

POWER. TO THE PEOPLE!

Are Your Abs Bullet-Proof?

Introducing the Ab Pavelizer— the fastest and safest way to a ripped powerhouse of six-pack muscle

In *Beyond Crunches: Hard Science. Hard Abs.* Pavel Tsatsouline reveals the Janda sit up, the world's most effective and safest abs exercise. Normally the Janda sit up requires a partner, for correct form. The Ab Pavelizer means you don't have to rely on a friend to develop eye-popping abs. Now, it's strictly between you and your abs. With as little as five reps a day, you can own the world— ABSOLUTELY.

Don't let anyone get between you and your world-class abs— order your Ab Pavelizer today— you'll turn heads and stop traffic every time you raise your shirt, we guarantee it.

Item # P8

This absolute ab machine is available in two versions:

The Ab Pavelizer (See photographs)
Easily fits under a door for a partner-free Janda sit up.
Item # P8 $119.95
(See the order form for shipping costs)

The Ab Pavelizer—Stand Alone (not shown)
The stand alone version allows you to attach a weight (you won't need more than 50 lbs.) to anchor the machine while you do your partner-free Janda sit up. You will not be able to fit this version under a door.
Item # P8A $159.95
(See the order form for shipping costs)

To Take Possession of Your New Abs
Call This Number Today: 1-800-899-5111

ORDERING INFORMATION

Customer Service Questions? Please call us between 9 am - 5 pm (CST) Monday - Friday at (651) 645-0517 or leave us a message any time for a prompt response.

100% One-Year Risk-Free Guarantee. If you are not completely satisfied with any product-for any reason, no matter how long after you received it-we'll be happy to give you a prompt exchange, credit, or refund, as you wish. Simply return your purchase to us, and please let us know why you were dissatisfied-it will help us to provide better products and services in the future. *Shipping and handling fees are non-refundable.*

Telephone Orders For faster service you may place your orders by calling Toll Free 24 hours a day, 7 days a week, 365 days per year. When you call, please have your credit card ready.

1-800-899-5111
24 HOURS A DAY
FAX YOUR ORDER (970) 872-3862

Complete and mail with full payment to:
Dragon Door Publications, P.O. Box 4381, St. Paul, MN 55104

✍ Please print

SOLD TO: *(Street address for delivery)* **A**

Name_____

Street _____

City _____-____

State _____ Zip _____

Day phone*_____
* Important for clarifying questions on orders

✍ Please print

SHIP TO: *(Street address for delivery)* **A**

Name_____

Street _____

City _____-____

State _____ Zip _____

Day phone*_____
* Important for clarifying questions on orders

ITEM #	QTY.	ITEM DESCRIPTION	ITEM PRICE	A OR B	TOTAL

HANDLING AND SHIPPING CHARGES
Total Amount of Order Add:

	$00.00 to $24.99	add $4.00
	$25.00 to $39.99	add $5.00
	$40.00 to $59.99	add $6.00
NO	$60.00 to $99.99	add $8.00
COD's	$100.00 to $129.99	add $10.00
	$130.00 to $169.99	add $12.00
	$170.00 to $199.99	add $14.00
	$200.00 to $299.99	add $16.00
	$300.00 and up	add $18.00

Canada & Mexico add $4.00. All other countries triple U.S. charges.

Total of Goods	
Shipping Charges	
Rush Charges	
MN residents add 7.8 % sales tax	
TOTAL ENCLOSED	

METHOD OF PAYMENT ❑ CHECK ❑ M.O. ❑ MASTERCARD ❑ VISA ❑ DISCOVER ❑ DINER'S CLUB ❑ AMEX

Account No. *(Please indicate all the numbers on your credit card)*   EXPIRATION DATE

☐☐☐☐ ☐☐☐☐ ☐☐☐☐ ☐☐☐☐   ☐☐/☐☐

Day Phone (   ) _____

SIGNATURE _____ DATE _____

NOTE: We ship all orders by USPS first class or priority mail. If you wish us to ship by UPS, we must have your street address. Foreign orders are sent by Air Printed Matter. Credit card or International M.O. only.

For rush processing of your order, add an additional $5.00 per address. Available on money order & charge card orders only.

ORDERING INFORMATION

Customer Service Questions? Please call us between 9 am - 5 pm (CST) Monday - Friday at (651) 645-0517 or leave us a message any time for a prompt response.

100% One-Year Risk-Free Guarantee. If you are not completely satisfied with any product-for any reason, no matter how long after you received it-we'll be happy to give you a prompt exchange, credit, or refund, as you wish. Simply return your purchase to us, and please let us know why you were dissatisfied-it will help us to provide better products and services in the future. *Shipping and handling fees are non-refundable.*

Telephone Orders For faster service you may place your orders by calling Toll Free 24 hours a day, 7 days a week, 365 days per year. When you call, please have your credit card ready.

1-800-899-5111
24 HOURS A DAY
FAX YOUR ORDER (970) 872-3862

Complete and mail with full payment to:
Dragon Door Publications, P.O. Box 4381, St. Paul, MN 55104

✐ Please print

SOLD TO: *(Street address for delivery)* **A**

Name_____

Street _____

City _____-_____

State _____ Zip _____

Day phone*_____
* Important for clarifying questions on orders

✐ Please print

SHIP TO: *(Street address for delivery)* **A**

Name_____

Street _____

City _____-_____

State _____ Zip _____

Day phone*_____
* Important for clarifying questions on orders

ITEM #	QTY.	ITEM DESCRIPTION	ITEM PRICE	A OR B	TOTAL

HANDLING AND SHIPPING CHARGES
Total Amount of Order Add:

	$00.00 to $24.99	add	$4.00
	$25.00 to $39.99	add	$5.00
	$40.00 to $59.99	add	$6.00
	$60.00 to $99.99	add	$8.00
NO	$100.00 to $129.99	add	$10.00
COD's	$130.00 to $169.99	add	$12.00
	$170.00 to $199.99	add	$14.00
	$200.00 to $299.99	add	$16.00
	$300.00 and up	add	$18.00

Canada & Mexico add $4.00. All other countries triple U.S. charges.

Total of Goods

Shipping Charges

Rush Charges

MN residents add 7.8 % sales tax

TOTAL ENCLOSED

METHOD OF PAYMENT ❑ CHECK ❑ M.O. ❑ MASTERCARD ❑ VISA ❑ DISCOVER ❑ DINER'S CLUB ❑ AMEX

Account No. *(Please indicate all the numbers on your credit card)*   EXPIRATION DATE

☐☐☐☐ ☐☐☐☐ ☐☐☐☐ ☐☐☐☐   ☐☐/☐☐

Day Phone (   ) _____

SIGNATURE _____ DATE _____

NOTE: We ship all orders by USPS first class or priority mail. If you wish us to ship by UPS, we must have your street address. Foreign orders are sent by Air Printed Matter. Credit card or International M.O. only.

For rush processing of your order, add an additional $5.00 per address. Available on money order & charge card orders only.

ORDERING INFORMATION

Customer Service Questions? Please call us between 9 am - 5 pm (CST) Monday - Friday at (651) 645-0517 or leave us a message any time for a prompt response.

100% One-Year Risk Free Guarantee. If you are not completely satisfied with any product-for any reason, no matter how long after you received it-we'll be happy to give you a prompt exchange, credit, or refund, as you wish. Simply return your purchase to us, and please let us know why you were dissatisfied-it will help us to provide better products and services in the future. *Shipping and handling fees are non-refundable.*

Telephone Orders For faster service you may place your orders by calling Toll Free 24 hours a day, 7 days a week, 365 days per year. When you call, please have your credit card ready.

1-800-899-5111
24 HOURS A DAY
FAX YOUR ORDER (970) 872-3862

Complete and mail with full payment to:
Dragon Door Publications, P.O. Box 4381, St. Paul, MN 55104

✍ Please print

SOLD TO: *(Street address for delivery)* **A**

Name_____

Street _____

City _____ -_____

State _____ Zip _____

*Day phone*_____
* Important for clarifying questions on orders

✍ Please print

SHIP TO: *(Street address for delivery)* **A**

Name_____

Street _____

City _____ -_____

State _____ Zip _____

*Day phone*_____
* Important for clarifying questions on orders

ITEM #	QTY.	ITEM DESCRIPTION	ITEM PRICE	A OR B	TOTAL

HANDLING AND SHIPPING CHARGES
Total Amount of Order Add:

	$00.00 to $24.99	add $4.00	Canada & Mexico add $4.00. All other countries triple U.S. charges.
	$25.00 to $39.99	add $5.00	
	$40.00 to $59.99	add $6.00	
NO COD's	$60.00 to $99.99	add $8.00	
	$100.00 to $129.99	add $10.00	
	$130.00 to $169.99	add $12.00	
	$170.00 to $199.99	add $14.00	
	$200.00 to $299.99	add $16.00	
	$300.00 and up	add $18.00	

Total of Goods	
Shipping Charges	
Rush Charges	
MN residents add 7.8 % sales tax	
TOTAL ENCLOSED	

METHOD OF PAYMENT ❑ CHECK ❑ M.O. ❑ MASTERCARD ❑ VISA ❑ DISCOVER ❑ DINER'S CLUB ❑ AMEX

Account No. *(Please indicate all the numbers on your credit card)*　　　　EXPIRATION DATE

❑❑❑❑ ❑❑❑❑ ❑❑❑❑ ❑❑❑❑　　　❑❑/❑❑

Day Phone ( )_____

SIGNATURE _____ DATE _____

NOTE: We ship all orders by USPS first class or priority mail. If you wish us to ship by UPS, we must have your street address. Foreign orders are sent by Air Printed Matter. Credit card or International M.O. only.

For rush processing of your order, add an additional $5.00 per address. Available on money order & charge card orders only.

NOTES

NOTES